Dear Linda,

Do not give up! When God closes a door he opens up a gate.
Perhaps your experience will help you to be a better ambassador
for peace and justice in Palestine.

May God's grace give you peace in this and in all situations . . .

Rev. Alex Awad
Dean of Students, Bethlehem Bible College
Palestine

01.02.10

Stephen,
It's an honour
to share my story
with a brother
in this journey
towards peace
+ justice

Linda

For the **Love** of Hamoudi

Dedication

To all the dreamers and believers out there . . .
you CAN do it! God has a whole pocket full
of miracles for us.

To my students in Gaza . . .
I am so grateful that I got to know you through
all of this. I love you so much.

And to my own children . . .
I couldn't have done any of this if you,
Zack, Celeste, Emily, Maddy and Sami, aren't
the amazing people that you are.
I love you so much I can't even
breathe sometimes.

For the **Love** of Hamoudi

Hamoudi

You are an inspiration and continually teach me
how to be a better person.

I love you.

For the **Love** of Hamoudi

Acknowledgements

Thank you, first and foremost, to God, Who makes all things possible, and never runs out of miracles when I need them most. He has taught me how to trust, how to have faith, and how to listen to His voice. His leading will forever change my life.

To my parents, thank you for all your support through so many things you didn't fully understand. Thank you for being generous even when you couldn't see the situation the same way that I did. Thank you so much for taking Hamoudi into our family and into your hearts as you have. It means so much to me for him to be taken into your embrace.

To my children, Zack, Celeste, Emily, Madeline, and Sami, who have helped me carry this burden all these years. I love you, and I will never have the words to fully express what you mean to me. Your love and strength have helped me to keep going through many difficulties and disappointments. I love you all so much.

To the rest of my family, I know this journey has been hard for you and, at times, frustrating and bewildering. Thank you for being part of shaping me through the years into the person I am today. God has a purpose for everything!

To my friends who were sure I had lost my mind, thanks for sticking with me! I appreciate your love and support even when my life and choices made no sense to you.

And to my beloved Hamoudi, this story would have never happened without you. You are the love of my life, my dream come true. By knowing you, I have learned how to pray in faith and trust God for the outcome. You are more precious to me than you will ever know. I love you with all my heart.

i

For the **Love** of Hamoudi

Introduction

As we rolled along that last piece of highway, I was filled with excitement and wonder. I saw the signs for Rafah and watched as the miles counted down. We were almost there! The bus was buzzing with conversations about whether or not we'd actually be allowed to cross the border into Gaza. We had spent months planning, and hundreds of dollars each to get this far, but now that we were here, there was still the distinct possibility that we wouldn't be allowed in.
I, however, could not contain my enthusiasm. I had believed all along that this was exactly where God had brought me, not to the brink of Gaza, but actually into Gaza.

I kept telling those around me that I was sure we would get in. They would give me a knowing smile, finding my naiveté to be so precious. I was told over and over again that it is very rare for the Egyptians to allow anyone to cross into Gaza, even with all the necessary permits. Our group was bringing playground equipment, some of which it had not cleared with the Egyptian authorities.

The experience of many on this bus was to come this far, all the way to the Rafah border which divides Egypt and Gaza, and then sit, maybe for hours, maybe for days. Maybe finally being allowed through, maybe finally to be turned back. The one sure thing was that we were going to sit.

The group leaders advised everyone to get off the bus; that it was going to be a very long day out in the north Sinai sun. I couldn't help but think to myself, "No, we don't need to. God is bringing me into Gaza. He didn't bring me here to sit in the sun."

I kept saying to my seatmate, "We're getting in! I'm so sure we're getting in!" As much as that's what everyone wanted, no one really believed it was going to be that simple.

I was sitting near the front of the bus so I had to be one of the first to disembark. I was sure I didn't have to do this because we were going to go ahead but I had voiced my feeling several times so now I just needed follow the rules.

I had barely stepped beyond the front edge of the bus when an Egyptian border guard walked quickly up to the small group of us who were first off the bus. He was waving his arms, as if trying to ward us off.

He stepped up to us and said, "Get back on the bus, we're opening the gate!

Suddenly, my mind was filled with the scene of Moses standing at the shore of the Red Sea, needing to cross but being sure there was no way through, until God split the sea in two!

Tears of joy filled my eyes as I hurried back on the bus, excitedly telling others as I rushed past, "They're opening the gate! They're opening the gate!"

It had been a long journey, a very long journey to get this far, and now the gate was opening and I was about to enter my destiny.

I had been traveling on this road to Gaza for nine long years, and finally, I was there! Join me on the journey!

Linda Todd Gharib

Table of Contents

For the **Love** of Hamoudi

For the **Love** of Hamoudi
my journey of faith into the Gaza Strip

by Linda Todd Gharib

Foundation
UNIVERSITY PRESS

AMSTERDAM | LONDON | SINGAPORE | SALEM

For the **Love** of Hamoudi
my journey of faith into the Gaza Strip

Foundation Press is the non-academic division of Foundation University Press.

Copies of this book may be ordered through booksellers or by contacting:

Foundation Press
Post Office Box 12429
1100 AK Amsterdam, The Netherlands

office@foundationuniversity.com
www.foundationuniversitypress.com

ISBN: 978-94-90179-10-6

cover illustration | Bryce Choquer   cover & book design | timmyroland.com

Chapter One

We Have Arrived!

Hamoudi sent this to my parents shortly before I crossed the border into Gaza . . .

Dear Mom and Dad,

I just got a message on my phone from Linda, she arrived safely to Cairo and she wanted to let you know so you can get in touch with the kids and tell them their brave Mom made it safely.

Linda and I are getting married the second she crosses the Rafah border, I hope we can make you proud, I love you and I thank you from the deepest part of my heart for making my dream come true, I know Linda wouldn't have made it if it wasn't for your help, I owe you my life for that.

Please don't worry about your precious daughter, I will put her in my eyes, I will treat her so good and I will protect her as well, I have loved Linda for almost 9 years now, and I know I will keep loving her forever, no one had ever done for me and my people what Linda has done over the years, the only reason I have made it in this cruel life was your daughter, and I'm willing to spend my life being grateful and showing it by actions, not words.

We will keep in touch and I will definitely send you some pictures of us together.

Thanks a million, your son,

Hamoudi

After passing through the gate on the Egyptian side of the Rafah border, we still had to go into the border terminal and wait for our passports to be processed. This took a very long time because there were almost one hundred of us in our group, and the Egyptian border agents were in no hurry to allow us to continue on our way.

As the hours passed, I found myself vibrating with excitement. Yes, we were now parked in the terminal waiting for what was obviously a delayed processing of our passports, but I didn't care. We were here. I was here! We had made it through the gate so now, no matter how long this took, it was only a matter of time until we passed through the doors into Gaza.

I kept thinking of Hamoudi. He was waiting for me on the other side. When the Egyptian border agent had sent us back onto our bus because they were opening the gate for us, I had called him with the good news. He was at least as excited as I was because the gate on the Gaza side was already open! They were waiting for us to arrive!

It was a surreal time for me. Eight years of waiting were about to come to an end. An impossible dream was about to be realized.

I had wished for this moment, prayed for this moment, and worked for this moment for so long that I had often wondered if perhaps I was aiming too high. Perhaps dreams this big didn't come true for regular people like me. And yet, there I was. It was really happening!

We **Have** Arrived

From the Egyptian terminal, we boarded another bus to take us through the no-man's land between Egypt and Gaza, and were brought to the door of the Gaza border terminal. As the bus approached the building, I could see Hamoudi standing there waiting for me. He was wearing a sky blue t-shirt with a black and white kuffiya (Palestinian scarf) wrapped loosely around his neck. As if needing to bolster his courage for this most remarkable day, Hamoudi's t-shirt read, "Just Do It".

Tears filled my eyes. We had loved each other for so long but had never seen each other in person. We'd never touched each other's skin, never felt each other's breath, but there he was, waiting for me – and I was finally there!

I don't remember anything else that was happening at that moment. I don't remember getting off the bus; I don't remember walking across the remaining distance between us.

I do remember wondering what I should say and not having the first clue what that should be. I didn't want to hesitate because I didn't want Hamoudi to misinterpret my hesitation as any kind of fear or regret. How can I assure him that I am thrilled to finally be with him and my lack of words is simply because I'm so excited? I came up with the perfect solution.

As soon as I was standing in front of him I threw my arms around his neck and we hugged. We hugged eight years worth of longing. We hugged eight years of missing each other; eight years of wondering if this moment would ever come; eight years of struggling against our own doubts as well as the doubts of those around us.

We stood, lost in each other's arms, and let the rest of the world carry on without us for those beautiful first moments together. We didn't say a word as we stood in each other's embrace. We didn't need to. The love we shared was enough as our hearts communicated everything we had lost the words to express.

Finally, he said, "Welcome to Gaza, baby"

His voice! I had only ever heard his voice over the phone and computer. I had never heard his voice clearly as I finally did, standing in front of him. I didn't realize how much of his voice I had missed. You really can't know what you miss when you haven't had it yet.

Make no mistake; we missed each other for all these years. We wanted to be together, but now that we were standing face to face I realized that I really hadn't known anything. If I could have known what I discovered in that moment, I don't think I could have survived being away from him all this time. My love for him rushed through my body and spirit like a river. My life would never be the same.

We were jolted back to reality with the overwhelming feeling that we were being watched. Hamas officers stood all around, staring at this curiosity. In Gaza, it's not generally accepted for men and women to express affection in public, and certainly not if they are not married to each other. But, since I was with the newly arrived group of humanitarian activists, a Code Pink delegation, they stood back and allowed us to have our moment.

Even so, I lost track of Hamoudi for a moment and as I look around to find him, I was shocked and scared when I saw him, many meters away, surrounded by angry looking bearded men. They were Hamas officers. I didn't know what to do, except I was sure that my running over there wouldn't help at all, so I just kept watching them. Eventually, they let Hamoudi come back to our group and I noticed the chain that I had sent him that he wore around his neck was dangling from his fingers. I thought it was broken.

"They broke your chain?" I asked in shock.

"No no, I just had to take it off", Hamoudi answered, a little breathless.

The Hamas officers were offended by his chain and forced him to remove it. It was my first taste of just how strict and conservative that life here could be.

We shook off the whole scene and went into the building where there was the entire local press waiting for us! What a great welcome!

There were cameramen and reporters from Reuters, AP, Xinhua and probably others, trying to get good footage of this visiting group of men and women who were braving the siege on Gaza to bring playground equipment to replace some of what was destroyed in the Israeli invasion six months prior.

In our last night in Egypt, in a small town called Al Arish, near the Rafah border, I had gone shopping with some of the other women and I bought a beautiful Arab dress to wear for our wedding. Yes, Hamoudi and I intended to marry when I arrived and I wasn't about to waste another minute!

I excused myself from the group and dashed into the washroom. I quickly changed out of my t-shirt and pants and threw on my gorgeous blue dress and pink scarf. Hamoudi had no idea what I was doing along with almost everyone else. Only a few women knew why I had disappeared.

When I came out of the washroom, gliding like a princess in my floor length, exquisitely designed gown, all of the cameramen suddenly ran from the ongoing press conference and rushed to photograph me!

5

Hamoudi was speechless, but soon found his voice and announced happily that we were going to get married! The room suddenly had a festive atmosphere, even more so than before. People started singing and cameramen suddenly became paparazzi as they shouted out "Linda!" "Hamoudi!" trying to get us to look at them so they could get their perfect shot.
I don't remember ever having that much fun! I felt like a movie star and kept smiling and laughing.

What a contrast! We were in the Gaza Strip; an area whose residents had been living under a crippling siege for about three years by then; an area where poverty and unemployment touched almost every family; an area that had been absolutely devastated only six months before we got there in a breathtaking military assault that had left about 1400 people dead in an operation that lasted 22 days. The suffering here is unfathomable but on that day, all we knew was our endless joy of finally being together.

Hamoudi had planned to bring a Mazoon (wedding officiate) to the border with him to marry us, but found out at the last minute that he wouldn't be able to. This wasn't the way they did things, apparently.

After so many years, he didn't want to wait any longer for us to get married. We wanted to run off and spend some time together but I had to stay with the group. Hamoudi was so disappointed and frustrated but he was very good about it and worked around our restrictions. He simply joined us on the bus.

As we sat, side-by-side, I couldn't take my eyes off him. It felt like a dream. I'd seen his face thousands of times online over our eight years, but never in person. It was amazing to see him. I felt like my mind must be playing tricks on me, but there he was, for real. We held hands. How good it felt to finally touch him! How good it felt to finally be held by him. There wasn't much we could say on that noisy crowded bus, but our eyes said everything as we just sat and stared at each other, gazing into each other's hearts and knowing everything we wanted to say.

He kept whispering, "I love you" over and over again. It was all I wanted to hear, finally in person.

Even as I write these words, I am taken back to that magical moment and I have to laugh. It was a perfect day.

Hamoudi and I had to part company as I continued on a tour with the group and he went back to work until I could be free later in the day.

We toured around and saw the destruction that was left from the recent attacks. It was overwhelming for me to finally witness Hamoudi's world with my own eyes. I had read about it, talked about it, wept about it, but I had never stood in the middle of it until that day. It was more terrible than I ever imagined.

The fact that my sweetheart had survived such a destructive assault made my stomach weak. He had been through so much, suffered so much. I was determined to love him enough to make up for all of his pain and loss.

I had no doubt that God had brought me through the many difficult circumstances in my life to prepare me to thrive in the place He had now put me. In Gaza, there was an endless supply of sand, dirt, rust and brokenness – how much I could relate! This could have been a description of me, at one point in my life. As I stood in Gaza, I felt the blessing of God wash over me. This was an amazing answer to prayer; almost more than I dared to ask for. But I asked, and here I was.

For the **Love** of Hamoudi

I saw the American International School on our tour, and it was flattened. The lineup of school buses completely burned out. It takes your breath away to see a school in this condition. I have children in school. It's supposed to be a safe place, a place of laughter and play. This school was another grim reminder of Gaza's suffering. I learned later that the school janitor had been in the building that night and he had been killed.

Our tour came to an end, and we headed back into Gaza City. I was eager to see Hamoudi again. Now that we'd been together, all I wanted was to be with him again.

Finally, we could be alone and we kissed for the first time. Believe me, a kiss that you've waited eight years for is a truly remarkable kiss! In an instant I knew I could never kiss any other lips. Every little detail was magical. We had waited so long and I couldn't help but realize that he was well worth the wait.

We had a meeting of everyone who had come on this trip in the dining room of the Commodore Hotel. It was a beautiful new hotel and the dining room had traditional fabrics and colours. I loved it!

Although I had talked on the phone to Hamoudi's brother, Omar, for years, I obviously had never met him in person either. When I arrived in the dining room, someone told me that a guy named Omar had been looking for me. I was so excited! Hamoudi's brother! Omar and I had spent many hours on the phone and I was thrilled to finally see him.

I looked around the room, having the advantage of knowing he was there without him knowing I was there, and scanned all the faces until I saw him.
Not wanting to be recognized, I kept my face turned slightly

and was careful not to make eye contact with him as I made my way around the room, ducking behind people every time Omar looked around.

My plan was working perfectly! No one else knew who I was because we were a fairly large group, having come from many corners of Canada and the US. I snuck around everyone in my way until I was right beside Omar. He was sitting and I was standing so he didn't notice me standing by him.

I suddenly lunged at him, grabbing his shoulders and said loudly "Hey Omar! I'm here!" Poor Omar! He almost died! He jumped and caught his breath. He was so surprised. The look on his face made my whole sneaky plan worth the effort. He jumped out of his chair and we hugged. Again, it wasn't as if we were hugging for the first time, it was as if it was a reunion.

I was home with my family. There was no mistake about that.

Prior to coming, I had been shy about telling a lot of people at home about our plans to marry because everyone has an opinion about people who meet someone online and run off to a foreign country to marry. When that foreign country is Gaza, people are sure you are nuts. In order to avoid those conversations, I hadn't talked about it in any definitive terms. I used words like "maybe" and "we'll see how it goes".

How could I expect them to understand the clarity with which God had been leading me all these years? Yes, I was in love with Hamoudi, but God had brought us together to teach me of His love for Palestine.

I was humbled and in awe of a God who goes to such great lengths to show His love and compassion, and that He had found me worthy to be part of this great plan.

From the first second I was in Hamoudi's arms, I had no doubts at all. I was definitely going to marry this man!

Now that I was with him, I regretted not being more sure of our plans, or at least, I regretted not having the courage to share it with everyone. I regretted being afraid of the criticism that I had endured.

When God speaks to one, He doesn't always reveal the plan to everyone else. He lays out a path for each one who follows Him. I wish we could all trust God enough to let each other follow His calling for them. Unfortunately, there are still many who are quick to criticize what they don't understand.

But that didn't matter anymore.

Hamoudi and I were together and we were going to get married the next morning. We had planned to marry as soon as I arrived, but since Hamoudi had learned it would be a bit more complicated than expected, we had to wait until the next morning.

Morning came and I was so excited! Today, Hamoudi and I would finally be married! I put on my pretty new dress and Hamoudi and I went to see the wedding officiate. We told him we wanted to marry, presented all of our I.D. and related paperwork, and waited with eager anticipation as he looked over everything.

I don't speak Arabic so I had no idea what this man was saying to Hamoudi, but I knew it wasn't good because Hamoudi didn't look as happy as a man should look who is about to marry the woman of his dreams. When they finally finished talking, Hamoudi told me that there was some other paperwork we needed to do before this man would marry us.

We **Have** Arrived

We left that office and ran around the city to other offices and paid for more certificates and stamps and applications. Everything is only written in Arabic so I wasn't sure of any of it, but since it had to be done, I didn't question it.

We made it back to the official's office before the end of a long, hot and hectic day, hoping to finally get married.

He looked at our new paperwork, which was everything he had told us to get. He started in on another long conversation with Hamoudi. I sat quietly by, nervously wondering what they were talking about. Hamoudi looked miserable. I didn't need to speak Arabic to guess what the news was.

Hamoudi was so frustrated as we left the office for the second time that day. This official decided that there was more paperwork and more approvals we needed before he would allow us to marry, but the other offices were closed for the day, so we'd have to try again the next day.

Even though it was only day two, it felt like forever. Getting married was supposed to be simple! Don't people run away to Las Vegas on the spur of the moment and get married? They don't need anything. They don't even need to know they were going to get married. They don't even need to know what they're doing. Here was Hamoudi and me, frantically running around town, paying office after office for some obscure stamps and whatever else he was told and we still didn't have enough to convince this man to marry us.

I got the feeling that he didn't like me very much. Here I was, this bold foreigner, coming to marry a local boy. I was sure he didn't think I was good enough for Hamoudi and was trying to discourage me.

When we had sat in front of his desk earlier, I crossed my

legs, as I normally do. He immediately muttered something angrily to Hamoudi who quickly advised me to put both feet on the floor. With my legs crossed, one of my knees was higher than the edge of the desk. I guess this was offensive to him, even with my long dress covering me to the floor.

I guess we just didn't get off to a good start because of this accidental cultural faux pas. Now we were going to pay for it.

The next morning we showed up at the appropriate offices, paying for all that had been required of us and again we ran back to the official's office.

This time, Hamoudi's dad's assistant came with us. Maher was part of the family and had been for several years. His work was all about red tape and paperwork so he took everything in hand and guided us through a second day of running around. Hamoudi and I were so frustrated and exhausted by this time that I am sure there is no way we could have gotten it done without our angel, Maher.

His warmth, kindness, sense of humour, and endless patience made all of these complications somehow bearable. He effortlessly guided us through the many stops we had to make that day, never seeming the slightest bit ruffled by any of it.

Maher didn't speak any English and I didn't speak more than a couple of words of Arabic, but we learned to understand each other, and it even made the day fun.

The word I seemed to get the most use of was "majnoon", which is Arabic for "crazy". It was that kind of day.

At long last, we had everything done! There was still time to make it back to the office where all of this madness had started. If he was happy, we just might end up married that day. If not, I was afraid we might never get married.

We finally got this sullen official's permission to marry! That meant we had to then run to another office to present ourselves to the Mazoon, who actually witnesses the vows. I learned that I needed a representative, someone to enter into the marriage contract on my behalf. What a strange world I had come to. Nothing was familiar to me.

Maher was still with us so he was declared to be my representative. He and Hamoudi sat opposite each other in front of the Mazoon and repeated to each other whatever they were instructed to do.

I received the following email from Hamoudi on May 18, 2009; two weeks before I arrived . . .

> *I love you, I love you, I love that you are my wife, I wont ever let you down wifey, making you happy will be my everyday task, and I will fulfill that task perfectly no matter what I had to do!*
>
> *Linda Todd, please accept my marriage proposal on the boarders, and become my wife, and I will live to satisfy you as long as I am breathing.*

I sat on the side, quite amused to watch all of this. I was the one getting married, but I seemed to have no part in the ceremony.

Hamoudi and Maher had to hold each other's hands through everything they recited to each other.

When it was finally all done, I asked Hamoudi if he was

now married to me or to Maher. It was funny for me to watch how all of this was done. Apparently, if Hamoudi ever leaves me, he has to pay me ten thousand Jordanian dinars or something like that. When the official asked us what the dowry was, Hamoudi turned to me and said, "Don't make it too high, I'm broke." We both started laughing and we were the only two in the room who knew why.

By the time we were finally married, I almost didn't care how it happened. As long as the day ended with us married, they could make me sign anything and I wouldn't care.

I was hot, sweaty and exhausted. We'd been trying for three days to get married after eight years of waiting, and after everything we'd been put through, it had definitely lost its romantic sparkle. We dragged ourselves back to Hamoudi's family's home and I said to his step mom, Hanan, "They sure know how to suck the romance out of getting married around here!"

She smiled and replied, "it's ok, the romance is for the marriage". I smiled, appreciating her calm reassurance. In Gaza, a little inconvenience is really nothing to complain about. Here, people learn to take everything in stride; delays, cancellations, red tape. All are just part of life here.

We had a party with the rest of the family that evening. It was so nice to be warmly welcomed in like this. Not only would my life never be the same, but neither would theirs. The day would come when Hamoudi would leave there and come to Canada to live with me and my children, of whom he was now their stepfather.

Hamoudi's tata (grandma) was the one I had to convince that I was the right one for her boy. She had helped to raise him since he was little and the love between them is very deep and strong. There would be trouble for me if tata didn't approve. She had watched Hamoudi's love for me grow over the years and she knew how much he loved me. When she and I met, she held my hand and kissed me. Hamoudi was overjoyed! I was in!

Some friends of Hamoudi's gave us the use of their flat to live in while I was there. It had a beautiful view of the city. Now that we were married we were finally able to enjoy living together! We ran to our flat as soon as the party was finished and enjoyed the beginning of married life.

We had an air conditioner in the bedroom that gave us relief from the suffocating Gaza heat. We nicknamed the bedroom "Canada" and the rest of our flat was "Gaza". We were able to escape to Canada anytime we needed to.

One of the members of the group I came in with was Norm Finkelstein. I really enjoyed getting to know him. While we were still in Egypt I told him I was getting married when I got to Gaza. He laughed and said, "It would have to be a man from Gaza to marry a woman who already has five kids. Family means so much to Gazans. You're very lucky"

Yes I am. God has given me so much. He brought me to this wonderful place, He gave me this wonderful man and He set me on a path that would change my life in ways that I only dreamed of.

Here's an email from my oldest son, Zack, when I told him I'd arrived safely . . .

> *Hey mom that's awesome to hear! I'm glad your somewhat safe haha those roads sounds pretty scary though! Stay safe and I look forward to hearing from you again!*
>
> *Love you,*
> *Zack*

For the **Love** of Hamoudi

Chapter Two

Wedded Bliss

We had our own flat! Here I was, not only in Gaza, not only married to the amazing love of my life, but we also had our own flat!! It was beautiful!

From the balcony, I could look out over Gaza City. To the right, I could see a huge collapsed building; it looked like a government building, right in the middle of town. I caught my breath as I imagined the moment it fell and how I would have felt, if I'd been standing here on my balcony on that day.

Our living room windows were broken with pieces missing from the blasts of the explosions during that invasion. Since glass was not allowed into the Gaza Strip, the windows in our flat, and every other flat, could not be replaced but only covered in plastic.

I saw the water tanks on every roof that I'd only ever read about. And I saw the holes that had been shot in so many. My heart ached as I thought of the kind of traumas my husband had suffered. As I stood in his world, I came to understand him so much more. My love for him grew and deepened. I felt protective of Hamoudi. I never wanted him to have to be alone in this nightmare. We were finally married and I would never let him be lonely again.

We had so much fun seeing his Gaza. Everywhere we went, Hamoudi held my hand. Our hands fit perfectly together, and we'd waited so many years to learn that, we made sure to make the most of every moment.

Being a newlywed is wonderful no matter where you are! Hamoudi took me everywhere with him.

Hamoudi was a journalist with Xinhua (a Chinese news agency) so we got to visit his office and I met everyone he worked with. I felt like I was back in elementary school and I brought my brand new doll for show and tell – except this time I was the doll!

I was intrigued to find so much warm hospitality and joy in a place where there is so much suffering. Of everything I'd read about Gaza, I didn't expect to find so much laughter.

Hamoudi's favourite place to eat is a little pizza joint on the main strip in town called Sami's Pizza. We ate some kind of pastries, some filled with some kind of meat and other filled with some kind of cheese. (I didn't know and I didn't ask. I just ate them!) These delicious pastries were only one shekel each, which is around thirty cents in Canadian money. We ordered a whole plate load and devoured them! Everything tasted better now that we were eating it together.

I loved watching how Hamoudi's lips closed around his next bite, I loved watching how he ate like it just might be his last meal.
We had eight years to catch up on and only three weeks to do so. I didn't want to miss anything.

I had the privilege of interviewing one of the doctors at the Al Nasser Children's hospital one day as well as the director of the Ahli Arab Hospital, a Christian hospital also in Gaza. Hamoudi had to work so he called a taxi and sent his brother, Omar to accompany me for my interviews.

Wedded Bliss

Our driver was a young man who used to drive for the previous government in Gaza. Khalid (not his real name) was only 24 years old. Two years prior, he had been kidnapped off the street by armed men. As we drove through the intersection where they had snatched him, he told me the story. He was taken to a nearby mosque and held for 15 hours where he was beaten repeatedly. He was shot in both legs. I saw the scars left by the bullets.

He had been about to get married but his wedding had to be postponed until he recovered. He told me that the men who had kidnapped and tortured him came to his hospital room to kill him but his mother was at his bedside that day and she argued with them for the life of her son and they left.

Khalid is now the father of a beautiful baby girl, but he will never be able to stand for long periods of time without excruciating pain in both of his legs. I fell in love with him immediately. He reminded me of my oldest son, Zack, a kind, gentle and intelligent boy.

When I went back to my flat at the end of that day, I wept for the agony of this sweet young man. Gaza was so welcoming and yet so harsh. The fear and anger that simmered under the surface were, at times, palpable, and yet never did stand alone. They were always mingled with the warmth and easy hospitality that defines Palestinians.

We arrived at Al Nasser Children's hospital and wandered around the grounds until we found our way in. The hospital administrator wasn't there but we were invited to look around by Dr. Mustafa Al Kahlout, the doctor in charge. He is a pediatrician at the hospital.

Dr. Al Kahlout graciously allowed me to visit some of the children in his care. I had brought some toys with me and felt like the Good Fairy as I stopped by each bed and handed a toy, either to each child or to their mother sitting closely by.

I was touched by the look of genuine gratitude in these mothers' eyes as I handed over the toys. Israel restricts the import of toys into the Gaza Strip, so these children were getting a very rare treat.

Dr. Al Kahlout gave me each child's story as I visited with them. The hospital was old with chipped paint everywhere. Walls had water stains and pipes and wires were visible. Everything was just very old and beyond being able to be brightened up to look clean and fresh.

Two of the babies who stand out in my mind were two of the tiniest patients here. One was a little boy and the other, a little girl. Both had some kind of immunity disorder, although the doctors were unable to pinpoint it. All they could be sure of is that these babies were slowly dying and they were helpless to stop it. Dr. Al Kahlout told me that it wasn't that he felt these babies' illnesses were incurable, it was due to the fact that the siege on Gaza was preventing much needed medical supplies from coming in, as well as preventing these very sick babies from getting out.

I choked back tears as I looked at these little ones. Babies are already so fragile, so much in need of protection, and these two, even more so.

I imagined how I would feel if they were mine. I had five babies, one of whom had been critically ill as a newborn. I had the privilege of living in a country where we are not denied adequate healthcare, and my daughter lived. Here in Gaza, parents are not so privileged. They and their children are constantly denied lifesaving treatments because of the restrictions placed on products coming into Gaza.

Wedded **Bliss**

Dr. Al Kahlout told me that these two, for sure, would not survive the siege unless it ended immediately. As I write this, around one and a half years later, Gaza is still under siege, so I have to assume that those two little ones are now angels, safe in the arms of God.

When I got home that evening, I told Hamoudi all about my day and found strength and comfort in his arms.

This was a dream come true. As much as that day was filled with heartbreaking stories, I was able to come home to my husband and let the stresses of the day be eased away.

I'd been waiting eight years for this, but now the days were ticking past much too quickly. I knew I would have to leave and go back home to Canada but how could I leave him? We had finally bridged the terrible distance between us and had found that life together was even more than we dreamed of. How could I go back across the border alone?

I shook off those thoughts. They were too unbearable to waste any of our precious time on. I was determined to just enjoy every minute we had.

Hamoudi introduced me to a snack that I called Peanut Butter Cheezies; because I had no idea what they were actually called (I still hadn't learned that much Arabic)

They were only two shekels a bag so we'd buy 2 or 3 bags of them and a couple of cans of Coke Zero and we'd sit at home and watch the DVD's that I had brought with me.

DVD's, or recorded media of any type, are also banned, so the new movies I brought with me were a nice treat for Hamoudi. Books are also not allowed, so I brought several for his sisters and brother.

The snacks and Coke Zero came through the tunnels from Egypt since they, too, are on the prohibited list of goods.

My imagination was stirred as I looked at the scrapes and dents in the pop cans, knowing that some young man had risked his life to drag this can and many others like it, through the tunnels that ran under the border between Gaza and Egypt at Rafah. Every week there is news of someone being killed in the tunnels, either by the tunnels getting bombed by Israel, or gassed or flooded by Egypt or by an accidental collapse or electrocution.

Nothing in Gaza can ever be taken for granted.

With every moment of joy, there is pain around the corner. With every moment of pain, there is joy around the corner.

One of my sources of learning about Gaza was Brother Andrew and Al Janssen's book, "Light Force". In it, they provide an in-depth look at the church in the Middle East with so many great details about the church and the people in Gaza.

While in Gaza, I had the privilege of attending the Baptist Church there. Hamoudi and I arrived early for the service and as we got out of the car and walked towards the door, I noticed, to my surprise, that the church was located directly across the street from a Hamas police station. Police officers leaned against the wall surrounding the church. I smiled politely and offered a quiet "Marhaba" (hello) as I walked past them.

Everything I did seemed like it was out of a dream. I felt like I had to be constantly pinching myself just to be sure that all of this was really happening.

Wedded Bliss

I had told Hamoudi all about Brother Andrew and had showed him the pictures from Light Force. I even brought my copy of the book with me that day, although I really didn't know why.

As we were sitting in our seats waiting for the service to start, I heard a bit of a commotion at the door. The entrance was behind where we were sitting so I was not going to turn around to see what was happening. I had grown up in church so I knew it was to be expected for people to be arriving right up until the time the service actually started, and even after that.

Hamoudi, however, had never been to church until that day so he was interested in everything that was happening. He turned to see what was causing the commotion, and suddenly said to me, "Brother Andrew's here". I smiled and said, "No he's not", but thinking to myself, "How would you know?" I only ever showed him a picture of Brother Andrew that was years old, and didn't even know if he'd paid much attention.

Hamoudi insisted that he was right, so I finally turned and looked. There was Brother Andrew! I had never met him before, but always wanted to. He was one of my heroes since I was a child.

I had secretly prayed that God would allow me to meet Brother Andrew, but felt silly about letting anyone know. It seemed so trivial compared to the bigger needs and concerns of a trip to Gaza. As I sat in church that day and saw that Brother Andrew had just walked in on the same day that I did made me feel like God had wanted to give me an extra special gift to let me know I was exactly where He wanted me to be.

I couldn't stop the tears of irrepressible joy that trickled down my cheeks. This was one of the highest highlights of this trip.

I jumped out of my seat and ran over to Brother Andrew with the biggest smile on my face. "You're Brother Andrew!" was the best I could think of in the moment.

He smiled, "Yes I am"

I was practically giggling like a child at Christmas. There was so much I wanted to say to him! His book had been life changing for me. How could I express all that he meant to me in the split second of time we had as he made his way to the front of the church?

"You're the reason I'm here!" I blurted out. He smiled and his eyes sparkled. "In your book you said we should come, so I did!"

He smiled and told me, before making his way to the front of the church, that we would talk after the service.

My heart was pounding as I took my seat beside Hamoudi. My list of God's miracles for me was getting longer! I had come half way around the world and made it into Gaza, then I married this wonderful man that I love so much, then I got to walk the streets of Gaza and see for myself all that is happening there, then I came to church and Brother Andrew was there on the same day!

As I sat down, going over all the reasons I was so excited, Brother Andrew was invited to the pulpit – and my day just got better! Brother Andrew was preaching that day!

After what was an amazing church service, Hamoudi and I were still in our seats talking to each other and visiting with others, when Hamoudi said, "Brother Andrew is calling you up there". Again, I said, "No he isn't". As I think of that day, I have to stop and laugh. Poor Hamoudi! Why I didn't believe him at all, I'll never know, but this was the second time that day he had unbelievable news for me and it was the second time I didn't believe him.

"Yes, he is calling for you, look!"

Finally, I looked to the front of the church and saw Brother Andrew motioning with his hand for me to go and talk to him. My heart jumped in my chest! He really did want to talk to me!

I hurried to the front of the room and was introduced to Al Janssen, Brother Andrew's colleague and co-author. He was eager to hear my story. What was a woman from Canada doing in Gaza? How did I come to be at this church?

They had a cameraman who traveled with them to document all of Brother Andrew's movements so he filmed the conversation I had with Al Janssen.

The excitement showed in his face as I told him what a powerful encouragement and influence their book had been for me. I told him about Hamoudi and our marriage and my life back home. He found it all very interesting.

Both Brother Andrew and Al signed my copy of their book. Finally I knew why I brought my book that day!

Those autographs have become one of my most precious mementos from my trip to Gaza. Those, and my marriage certificate, of course.

Another special gift

On one of my days in Gaza, our group went to visit the Jabaliya Rehabilitation Centre. This was a place that addressed the needs of the many people who had lost limbs during the recent attack, called Operation Cast Lead.

As we entered the room and greeted the many people who were still recovering from their injuries, I suddenly had a renewed sense of horror for what they had suffered.

One by one they told us their stories of where they had been at the moment the invasion changed their life forever. It was hard to watch and to allow myself to fully comprehend the nightmare they had lived through.

There were men, women, youths, children, just as you would find anywhere. Again, I paused and allowed my imagination to take me back to those terrible days Seeing their injuries gave us all a renewed commitment to spread the word of peace and justice for the people here in Palestine. The suffering in Gaza is overwhelming.

My observation remained true: With every moment of joy, there is pain around the corner. With every moment of pain, there is joy around the corner.

I was overwhelmed with the sight of so many amputees. I had to step out of the room. They didn't need to see my tears. The pain was theirs, not mine. I made my way to the door and stepped out into the hallway and took a deep breath.

"God, why is there so much pain here? What can I do?" I quietly prayed as I regained my composure.

I started looking around, trying to see what else this building was used for when I noticed some strange looking pictures hanging on the wall above the stairway leading to the upper floor.

Wedded Bliss

They were a series of pictures of children, each with one word on it. The children were all holding their hands differently. I'd never seen pictures like these.

I stared at the pictures, searching for their meaning as I looked back and forth, from one to the next all the way down the row.

Suddenly, like a flash in my mind, I figured it out! The children were using sign language! The pictures were writing out the name of the school for the deaf that occupied space upstairs! I almost ran up the stairs, unable and unwilling to contain my excitement.

I had worked with deaf children at home since I was 15 years old and continued to have contact with many deaf friends.

Years ago, I had discovered the existence of a school for the deaf in Gaza but had never been able to establish any contact with them. I had tried through several different channels, and for many years, but to no avail. There I was, getting closer with each stair that I leaped past.

I found the classroom at the top of the stairs and paused for a minute to watch the children. My heart was soaring! God had brought me to the doorstep of Gaza's school for the deaf! It was another special miracle just for my enjoyment.

I introduced myself to the teacher, Mohammed Muhaisen, and explained that I was from Canada and had worked with deaf children since I was quite young. The children had all stopped what they were doing to look at this strange foreigner who had interrupted their day.

"How do you say "I'm happy to meet you" in Arabic sign language?" I asked Mohammed suddenly. He slowly showed me all the signs then I turned my attention to the class and repeated what he had shown me. The children's eyes lit up. This foreigner was speaking their language!

With the teacher's help and a little bit of "relay signing", I managed to tell the students that I was from Canada and had worked with deaf children for many years.

They were amazed. "There are deaf people in Canada?" came from a shocked looking teenaged boy.

The children were so happy to learn that there were young people just like them in a country like Canada. They had no idea such a thing would be. I immediately took the opportunity, with the help of their teacher, to tell these children that they were just like children in Canada, and everywhere. I wanted to them to feel that they were part of something greater, and not so isolated, even though it feels that way in this lonely strip of sand on the shore of the Mediterranean Sea.

Before I left, they taught me how to say "friend" in their language so as I took my place back on the bus, a large crowd of deaf children gathered and signed "friend" to me. It was another moment of overwhelming joy found just around the corner from so much pain.

I was falling more and more in love with Gaza with every encounter I had with her people.

After I was in Gaza for several days, I received an email from my brother back home that broke my heart. In these days, I had witnessed incredible destruction that took my breath away. I visited with the sick and the injured. I had listened to Hamoudi's stories and to those of his family. I saw the pockmarked buildings in his neighbourhood, scarred from being shot at from Israeli helicopters. I had looked around enough to imagine what it might have been like to have lived through the most recent invasion.

As we sat at home in the evenings, there was always the sound of distant tank fire and bombing somewhere. I learned to stop and listen and identify from which direction the sounds came, and from which type of weapon. I never expected to know that.

When I saw I had an email from my brother, I was very happy. It had been awhile since I had last heard from him.
Upon opening it, my heart sank. It was a message that he was forwarding that had been designed to incite fear and hate toward Muslims. The email had done its job. My brother was acting in the intended fear inspired by such an email.

Jesus tells us to act in love – whether to our friends or our enemies. In this sad and broken place I had found, His love was needed more than anything.

I wrote back and begged him to stop sending such things. I told him that I was sitting in the middle of the devastating effects of hate and fear and I was pretty sure there had been enough of both of those to go around. We need to start spreading the message of hope, peace and reconciliation. This land and all the people here desperately need it.

It was a very happy day when my brother finally offered his support for what I'm doing. One step at a time we can break down the walls that imprison us and be free to reach out to each other.

I was blessed with Palestinian hospitality and kindness that made me wish I could bottle it and take it home with me on the day that Hamoudi took me out to his father's garden.
Hamoudi's father, Adnan, has a beautiful garden outside of

town where he would go to unwind and free his mind and spirit from the burdens of life under siege. Maher, his father's assistant, also came with us that day.

In this space, Adnan grows a variety of flowers, fruits and vegetables. His Palestinian olive trees are the obvious pride of his garden. When we came to the olive trees, he stopped and lovingly fingered the leaves as he showed them to me. I could sense a reverence in his demeanour as he stood and communed with these ancient citizens of the land.

As we were walking down one of the rows of this remarkable garden, my foot suddenly got stuck in some very thick mud and, to my surprise, my sandal broke! I started laughing, trying to figure out how I would get out of there without my foot becoming completely covered in dark, sticky mud when Maher, without missing a beat, kicked off his sandal and pushed it under my foot. He pointed at it and then at my foot and nodded. He then slid off his other sandal for me and turned to go back to the garden shed to find a spare pair of old shoes for himself.

I was moved deeply by this unselfish act of servant hood. If only those of us who claim to follow the Servant of All could grasp this beautiful attitude of a giving heart. What I saw in Maher that day has stayed with me until now.

This was the second time I witnessed the genuine humility, grace, dignity and unselfish hospitality in this man, who truly reflected Palestinian culture. When we never get out of our homes to go and visit those in other lands – and especially those in Palestine who are so maligned, we can never experience the blessings that are found when we allow ourselves to truly encounter other human beings. There is so much we can teach each other and learn from each other but we won't be able to do any of it if we never get to know each other.

Wedded Bliss

If I, a divorced single parent, could travel to Palestine and come face to face with another culture and people and learn who they really are, anyone can do it. Perhaps not everyone is being called to Palestine; perhaps someone's calling is to have a face-to-face encounter with someone else, somewhere else. Wherever you need to go, please go. We need to stop sitting smugly in front of the evening news passing judgment on people we don't know.

We don't need special skills to love and care for others. We just need an open and willing heart and enough compassion to withhold our judgment and let the love of God flow through us to others. We can't love those we don't bother to get to know.

Maher is Palestinian. He's not a terrorist. In fact, for anyone who took the time to get to know him, they would find that he is a good husband, a loving father and a kind and gentle man. And yet Maher and his family are among the million and a half Palestinians who are constantly subjected to a crippling siege, ensuring that they never have enough of their daily necessities and never have the security of knowing they'll be treated if they get sick, or to be able to travel if they need to go anywhere.

He gave me his own shoes without a second thought when I broke mine.

My early days of married life were already proving to be life changing. I didn't have to wait for the years to pass and the lessons to come with old age and the wisdom of advanced maturity. My life had already changed and was continuing to change minute by minute.

Every new experience Hamoudi introduced me to, he held me by the hand, always keeping me close. After so many years of loneliness it felt so good to be wanted this much.

Our intimacy was reflected in every look and every touch. Every tiny bit of contact between us was further evidence of the deep and loving intimacy we shared. We had known each other for years. Our marriage did not start on my third day in Gaza, our marriage started years before as our hearts had become one in a mystery that was written in the heavens before we ever found each other.

July 30, 2007

Dearest Wife Ever,

I have got myself into a lot of trouble winning this competition!!!! Now I have to write you emails every time I'm on here!!!! Don't worry though, I will not forget, I love you sweetie, my day has been so long because I didn't hear your voice a lot, I miss you like crazy, I got both your emails and you are hilarious, and I also got the letter you sent to that school! I love how you take care of me and you discuss our future with your kids, I hope they like me enough; God knows how much I love them and want to be their good daddy!

Baby I'm gonna send this to both your home and work addy, I love you Linda, please try to call me I miss you so much baby!

Your hubby, Hamoudi your champ!!

Chapter Three

Why go after 8 years?

It was amazing that after eight years of waiting and wanting, I was finally in Gaza. Why now? Hamoudi and I had met in the summer of 2001 and finally, in May 2009, I crossed the border. All I can say is that it was God's timing. There are reasons for everything.

I had tried to cool our relationship at times over the years. It just seemed too impossible. I was a single mother and my youngest child was only two years old when Hamoudi and I met. Travel was impossible for either of us.

Getting together wasn't an option but neither was letting go, no matter how hard I tried at times. It was as if God tied our hearts together in such a way that nothing could ever release us from each other. I had even tried dating others, to let Hamoudi go on with his life and to let me go on with mine. Always in the back of my mind and filling my heart was Hamoudi. I compared everyone to him. Under such a comparison, no one could ever take his place.

I prayed about this and begged God to make some sense of it for me. How do I spend my life with someone I can't spend the afternoon with? God didn't answer my question, but neither did He let my love for Hamoudi drift away.

For the **Love** of Hamoudi

We were connected in such a deeply spiritual way that even when we weren't talking, we still knew what was happening with each other.

We would call in a panic, "Are you alright? I just had a bad feeling that something was wrong!" And we were always met with a story of some difficulty we were facing at that moment and all we wanted was to hear from the other.

We were connected in a way that was so much bigger than either of us, so much more mysterious than we were able to comprehend, but definitely in a way that was of great comfort to both of us.

We spent most of 2008 in a cooler phase of our relationship. Hamoudi was working hard and pursuing his career in Gaza and I was working hard, trying to figure out my career. I was working as an administrative assistant for a federal government agency. I knew I wanted more. I believed God had shown me a very different path and I had believed that path included Hamoudi, but at this time, I couldn't figure out how all of that would work.

People were questioning my motivation for my work for Palestine, saying it was only because of Hamoudi; so I felt that I needed to prove them wrong by backing away from our personal relationship, and continuing to champion "the cause". People around me began to take me more seriously, but it was a hollow victory. My heart longed for Hamoudi, but my intellect told me that this was a better way.

Finally, in late December 2008, Hamoudi called me. "I don't know if you care or not, but turn on your news. They're dropping bombs on us. I don't know if it matters to you, but I wanted to tell you I love you. I don't know if I'll survive this time."

Why **Go** After 8 Years ?

I was startled! What was he talking about? I ran to the TV and found some news, which was broadcasting a heavy Israeli military invasion of Gaza. Bombs were dropping all over; white phosphorous was raining down on the city. It looked like a scene from an apocalyptic movie. I choked back tears and tried to find the words to express what was racing through my heart and mind. What if this was it? What if he didn't survive? Could I live with him dying without me telling him how much I love him?

I quickly realized that Hamoudi was the one I couldn't live without. I've often heard it said that we shouldn't marry the one we can live with; we should only marry the one we can't live without, and for me, that was Hamoudi. The problem was, his survival was completely out of my hands. All I could do was to sit and helplessly watch the news, day after day, and hold my breath, praying that somehow, God would wrap His hands around my beloved Hamoudi and let him live another day.

Being a journalist, it was Hamoudi's job to be out in the streets filming the stories of the dead and wounded. Everyday he would walk through the hospitals lined with women and children, often having to step over bodies as he made his way through to tell the story of this horror that his people were living through.

Every night I would call him and let him unload his heavy burden onto me. I heard countless stories of how many dead he had counted that day, how many injured and the gruesome nature of the injuries he saw. I could hardly breathe as he spoke, stifling my own tears as I let him share his pain with me. My heart was breaking. His experience was so far outside of my own. I had no way to absorb all of this horror; no reference point to help me cope. But he needed me to be strong enough to listen and not to make him carry it alone.

He told me of a neighbour of his, a woman, who had been at home when white phosphorous, was dropped over her street. The canister had gone through the window of this family's home, and the fire exploded onto this woman's leg. I sat shaking as he spoke, not knowing how to respond. What do you say? He needed to tell me and I needed to listen.

While people around me were casually going on with their lives, I was living the assault on Gaza every single day. For me, there was no "normal".

With each call I was sure I couldn't bear anymore, but then I would hear the sadness and fatigue in Hamoudi's voice and I knew that if he was to survive this, he needed me to stand with him all the way. I just kept praying that God would steel my nerves and my heart and give me the strength I needed to be a support for Hamoudi. His world was falling apart around him; he didn't need me to do the same.

There was no one who could relate to this nightmare so I had only God to lean on as I continued to absorb Hamoudi's agony every night. God is so good. He continued to give me the strength I needed everyday to keep from being overwhelmed by the stories I was hearing.

I kept praying for Hamoudi's survival, feeling guilty as I did because of the many hundreds who were falling as the weeks passed. I continued to pray. Hamoudi wasn't simply someone I felt I could live with. He was the one I knew I could not live without.

I have never felt as helpless as I did in the weeks of that invasion, which lasted into January 2009. The ceasefire was declared on the evening of Hamoudi's birthday. When it finally ended and Israel brought its troops home, I had an overwhelming knowledge that there could be no more delays, no more second thoughts. How long could I expect to put off what I knew was God's plan for me and expect Him to remain patient?

Ok God, I'm ready.

It was a simple prayer, but it started a chain of events in motion that would finally bring me half way around the world. After eight years, I was faced with the harsh reality of just how fragile life in the Gaza Strip is and that there are no guarantees of a tomorrow for anyone.

By this time, my youngest child, Sami, was ten years old and willing and able to stay in the care of my eldest son, nineteen year old Zack. My three daughters, seventeen year old Celeste, fifteen year old Emily and thirteen year old Madeline were more than capable of helping to keep Sami in line while I went away for a couple of weeks.

I still didn't have the financial means to make a trip like this happen, and I had no idea how I was ever going to get into Gaza. However God's voice had been unmistakable and it was time for me to go.

I came up with a revolutionary approach to the question of how I was to make all of this work out. I wouldn't do anything! If I really did hear God's voice about going to Gaza then I needed to trust that He also had the way for me to get there. There needed to be less of me worrying and more of me trusting Him.

I started asking around to see if anyone knew of any groups that were planning to go to Gaza. My personal contacts were limited, so I began to exercise my networking skills to find information that was, until then, out of my reach.

For the **Love** of Hamoudi

The first person I asked was a good friend of Hamoudi's who had also become a good friend of mine, Jon Elmer. He is a Canadian journalist who had traveled to Gaza and met Hamoudi. They became very close friends. Hamoudi told Jon all about me so the next time Jon was in Canada, we found each other. The day I met Jon was the closest I'd ever been to Hamoudi. Jon had hugged Hamoudi and as I hugged Jon, it was as if my spirit was carried across space and time and found its way to Hamoudi's arms.

Jon told me to look for a group called Code Pink, but to also ask around and see what others would say.

As I began asking, I kept hearing that same name. Code Pink. Everyone I asked gave me the same reply. Code Pink. If I were actually going to get into Gaza, I would have to learn more about this group that everyone else seemed to know about. Code Pink.

I finally learned that Code Pink was a women's American anti-war movement. Many men were also part of this very passionate group. I immediately got in touch with them and put my name on the list of the group heading out to Gaza at the end of May 2009. I told everyone that I was going and assured them that God would get me there!

It was a most amazing time for me to watch how God moves. Within a period of under three weeks, I had my name on Code Pink's list, my hotel in Cairo was arranged, I had a plane ticket and all that was left to do was to count down the days until it was time to finally embark on a trip of a lifetime and hold my beloved Hamoudi for the very first time.

Hamoudi was so excited. He couldn't believe that we were finally going to be together. It had been a very long road for him too. In many ways, it had been longer for him. He had survived more than just the recent invasion. There had been so much more that Hamoudi had suffered over the years, and he always had to come home alone. Although I, too, didn't have the comforts of a spouse, I did have my children who are a great source of companionship, family, and entertainment.

While nothing can replace your spouse in your life, my children certainly have kept my life full.

I got this message shortly after the invasion started

> **Hamoudi sent you a message.**
> **Re: Hey you!**
>
> **"I love you, and you know that more than anything! I'm alive and I will fight till the last breath."**

It was a surreal feeling to know that I was actually going to Gaza. It was impossible, but it was happening. It seemed that there was no shortage of miracles for Hamoudi and me, and I had let go of all thoughts of what could go wrong, or that with every peak, there must be a valley or that with every moment of joy, there is pain around the corner.

As Hamoudi and I saw our days together coming closer to reality, we talked about our next plans. Our hearts were breaking at the undeniable fact that I would soon be returning to Canada but we did our best to focus on more positive matters. We talked about Hamoudi's immigration, the baby we wanted to have, how much fun it would be for Hamoudi to take our two boys snowboarding on the local mountains once he had joined us.

We talked about anything to squash the growing dread in our hearts at having to face the inevitable.

One of the positives that I enjoyed thinking about was how amazing it was that this Hamoudi who I was now married to and living with was the same Hamoudi I had known all these years from a distance.

It was very gratifying to be able to look at him and know that I was right about him. I had friends that doubted and tried to discourage me from continuing my personal relationship with him. I had friends who spoke in terms of their "concern" but it always felt like they didn't respect my ability to get to know someone and certainly didn't respect the possibility that this was the way that God was leading me and Hamoudi was part of that.

All of their disapprovals were completely irrelevant now as I basked in the glow of a love that had overcome all the odds and oppositions. Together, Hamoudi and I were happier than either of us had ever been on our own.

There is pain around the corner

The day finally came when I had to pack my bags and get ready to go back to the border at Rafah. It seemed impossible. Hamoudi and I couldn't even look at each other as I packed. We both knew that the slightest glance would reduce both of us to tears. Somehow I had come to believe that this moment wouldn't have to come. But here it was.

I wanted to leave him all the clothes that I had worn that he loved so much. I left him my wedding dress. I couldn't bear to leave and take everything so it would look like I'd never been there. With every item I packed in my bag, my heart grew heavier and my tears came closer to falling. It was hard to believe this was actually happening. After everything it took to get me here, I was now preparing to leave. My mind was caught between numb and racing as I tried my best to cover the emotions that were surging inside me. There were no words to express my feelings so I silently continued.

We took the long hot taxi ride to the border, silently, desperately holding on to each other's hands. The agony in Hamoudi's eyes was more than I could bear, but what choice did I have? My children hadn't been prepared for me to stay longer than I already had, and it was much too soon for anything to have been done with Hamoudi's immigration application. All we could do was to be brave and know that we would work on being back together as soon as possible. It sounded nice and should have been comforting, but the reality of us having to be apart after waiting eight years to be together was so painful that nothing could make it bearable at all.

We finally arrived at the Rafah border and waited. Waiting is something that Palestinians are very good at. They are always waiting for something. Nothing can ever be taken for granted. They waited at borders, waited at roadblocks, waited for money to get to the bank so they could be paid, waited for another shipment of whatever it was they found last time they were in the store but couldn't be sure when they'd find it again. Yes, waiting was as much a part of life as any of the many things that caused suffering here and for Hamoudi and me, waiting for me to leave was almost laughable, if it wasn't for the fact that we both wanted to cry. Laughable because neither of us wanted it and yet here we were, putting ourselves through this.

I was worried about my children and I was worried about my job. I had to return so we didn't lose my income. I had spent so many years practicing swallowing the depth of my feelings for Hamoudi that I thought I could bury my feelings again just long enough to be able to leave without falling apart.

After we'd been at the border for a few of hours, we were finally told that the Egyptians refused to allow me to cross back out of Gaza. No reason was given, just a refusal. Even though that meant I would miss my flight and I'd need to re-book it, it was such a huge relief for Hamoudi and me. Neither of us had to take responsibility for me not leaving. It was out of our hands completely.

We couldn't hide our relief and joy at being given, what felt very much like, a stay of execution. We would be together for at least a couple of days more due to the time it would take to arrange for another flight. We rushed back home and held each other for so long. We wanted to make the most of the few precious hours extra that we'd been given.

The next two days went past much too quickly, but we were very much aware that we had been given something special. Once again, God had intervened on our behalf and spared us from the agony we couldn't face on the day I was supposed to leave. We had been given a chance to face the reality of my departure and a bit of time to get used to it.

Hamoudi's friends, Nabil and his wife, Wesam, learned of our situation and Wesam asked if she could travel with me when I finally did leave. Wesam was a local news anchor, and her agency had arranged for her to go for a training course in Dubai, so she had to go to Cairo for her flight.

The four of us traveled together to the border. I was relieved that Hamoudi had his friend with him this time. Once I left, he would need some comfort. I just didn't know any other way for us to do this at this time. I had to go back and he was unable to join me.

Again, we waited for hours. The border agents kept going back and forth with Wesam's ID and paperwork. Nabil and Hamoudi talked to the border agents. I wasn't sure if that was going to make any difference for either me or Wesam, but there is so little that anyone can do that will actually make any difference at the border, you find yourself trying to at least look like you might be having some effect on your day's outcome.

Wesam and I sat in the shade and talked about our plans for the day. We talked of what we would do in Cairo, where we would eat, what we might look at while we're waiting for our flights. We talked as if everything that was happening was perfectly normal. Every time Hamoudi and Nabil would walk back over to us, our eyes would meet and our pain would bring all of our thoughts to a sudden stop before we would force ourselves to continue on with the day's business.

Finally the Hamas border agent informed us that Egypt had given permission for me to leave Gaza but not for Wesam. There was no reason given, just that she would not be traveling that day. I wanted to give her my spot, but that's not how the border was managed. I suddenly felt all alone and I realized I was the only one of our little group who would be getting on the bus. I had been comforted by the fact that Wesam would be coming with me but with this surprise news from the border agent (a surprise to me but to no one else) I felt lost.

Hamoudi walked me to the door of the bus and quietly told me to get on. We had hugged each other over and over again at home because we knew we had to be careful about hugging in front of all these security officers. We didn't have the protection of the Code Pink delegation as they had left days ago.

I couldn't breathe. I couldn't think. I wanted to hold Hamoudi tightly and never let him go. We had waited eight years, through many invasions, many terrors, horrors, and many brushes with certain death. We had endured so many fears and agonies and had spent only twenty days to try to heal the wounds that both of us bore.

For the **Love** of Hamoudi

It wasn't enough time. There was so much more to say and to do. Neither of us could bear the thought of another eight years apart and our only hope was that we were sure we would be together again in a matter of months. It was a small comfort, however, because now that I had held Hamoudi, kissed him, had his scent lingering on my clothes, I didn't know how I would last a day without him. Spending the next few months without him was unthinkable.

I held onto his hand as long as I could as I slowly boarded the bus.

We waved at each other while we were still in sight and finally the bus took me away from my beloved husband and I was on my way back into Egypt.

June 15, 2009
My sweetheart,

I am at Nabil's, its almost 11pm Monday the 15th and I'm having a meltdown, I didn't know I will miss you that much baby, I cant breathe Linda, I couldn't stay in my room for one minute when I got back from the borders, I quickly changed and went out, I wandered in the streets till Nabil called me and asked me to come over for the night cuz Wissam and the kids are at her parents'

I will email your parents right now to let them know you have reached Cairo safely and I will email them again after I hear from you when u get to Amsterdam

Linda, you are my air, my heart, my soul, I just realized today that I can't ever go on without you baby. You are my everything. The sadness in my heart shows on my face so much that whenever people see me they tap on my back and ask me to hang in there, my tears are falling right now as I feel a stab inside my heart that's

44

Why **Go** After 8 Years ?

killing me from not being with you

I love you my beloved wife and I shall love you forever and ever yet to come

always yours,
Hamoudi, your husband

When I got back to the Egyptian border terminal, I expected to simply be allowed to leave. Hamoudi had arranged for a driver he knew to be waiting for me on the other side to safely transport me back to Cairo. He had instructed the driver to call him as soon as he had me in his car.

When I showed my passport to the border agents, they told me to sit down. There were a few other people, Palestinians, who were traveling that day and one by one, their passports were returned and they were sent on their way.
I was kept in the terminal.

Occasionally, one of the men would call me over and ask me where I was going, where I had been, had I been with Code Pink? The questions were often repeated and I didn't understand what the problem was. I hadn't given them an address for staying in Egypt because my plan was to go straight to the airport for my flight, which was later that same night.

I saw the border agents passing my passport back and forth between them, taking it into one of the offices and then into another. Eventually, I was the only traveler in the terminal that seemed to be bustling with border security agents.
I couldn't figure out what was so interesting about my passport or me, but it kept getting passed around. I was trying not to panic. From inside the terminal, I couldn't contact Hamoudi in Gaza or my embassy in Cairo. I was invisible. No one could reach me. I started to pray.

For the **Love** of Hamoudi

I kept getting asked the same questions so I kept giving the same answers regarding how I got into Gaza but finally, one agent asked why I had no address in Egypt. This point had finally raised their suspicions. I explained that my flight was that night so I was going straight to the airport, that I had no need of a hotel.

I didn't speak Arabic and the agent spoke very little English, so I used a lot of gestures and repeated single words to try to explain my situation. "Me. Plane. Today. No sleep Egypt. Plane today. Me no Egypt. Plane. Today." I just hoped I was making myself clear.

He asked to see my ticket. My heart sank. My ticket was printed with the date from 2 days before this when I was supposed to be on the plane. I didn't have access to a printer so I had just scribbled out that date with a pen and wrote in the new one. Would he accept that these were valid travel arrangements?

In that moment, I remembered the words of Brother Andrew that he used to pray as he was passing the borders to take Bibles into communist countries so long ago. He used to ask that God, who could make blind eyes to see, to, at this time, also please make seeing eyes blind.

I took a deep breath and held up my paper and pointed to the flight time and prayed he wouldn't see the pen marks on the paper.

He only looked at the time of my flight and ignored the date completely. "Oh yes, tonight", he said, and that was the end of that conversation.

They kept me waiting a little longer before letting me exit into Egypt. I had been in the terminal a little over three hours by that time. Hamoudi was very anxious because his friend had not found me yet and no one knew where I was.

As soon as we were in the car, the driver called Hamoudi and let us talk. It was so good to hear his voice, although it was disappointing for us to be back on the phone again.

Hamoudi checked up on me all the way to Cairo. He called every hour or so of that long six-hour drive. Egypt is a very militarized country so there are checkpoints all along the highways. Sometimes you will have to produce your passport and an explanation of why you are there and where you are going and sometimes you will just be waved through. The intensity of the scrutiny depends on which direction you're heading. If you're on your way to Cairo, it's not too bad, but if you're on your way towards the Gaza border, look out. I was to learn later just how intense the scrutiny could be.

The drive back to Cairo was fairly uneventful. We stopped to eat, to drink, to use the washroom and to simply take a break from the car. Finally, I was delivered to the airport where I waited for my flight home.

I had no words to describe how sad and lonely I was at that point – or how torn I was. Behind me was my husband, the love of my life. In front of me were my children, the other loves of my life. In that moment, I couldn't have both nor could I live without either. There are times in life where there really is no right place to be.

I prayed for the strength and wisdom to continue on this path that God had put me. I hadn't realized it would become this painful, however, even if I had, I would have had no choice but to follow it anyway.

I was on my way back home.

For the **Love** of Hamoudi

Chapter Four

Who said I was up for this?

I've asked myself many times, Why me? Sometimes I feel like Moses when God called him to do great things. Moses felt so inadequate. He was sure that his brother would be better for the job than he was. I'm not so sure I'd volunteer my brother for this life, but for sure, most days I feel very inadequate and would gladly hand it over to someone else.
I couldn't possibly have known, years earlier, that God was preparing my heart and my nerves for the life He would guide me into.

I had been in a difficult marriage for nine years. We had four beautiful children, one boy and three girls. I was never good enough, never did enough, never contributed enough. I became a foster parent because I thought this would be a good way to prove my worth. I knew I was a great mother, even if I did fall short in some other areas. If I could parent "professionally", then surely this would be my validation. However, my state of mental health had been eroding greatly over time and finally gave way.

In the aftermath of our separation, my ex husband filed for full custody of our children, citing my unreliability as grounds for me to lose them. It wasn't that I was unreliable; it was that I was unwell due to years of struggle. He won and I lived alone after being a stay at home mom for years.

I was broken, having lost everything that was precious to me. My children had been my whole world and now I was only

able to visit them on specified days, as if I posed some kind of threat. If I had been a drug addict or an alcoholic then I could have understood the restrictions, but I was just sad and lonely and isolated. How all of that translated into being an unfit mother, was beyond me.
I was thrust out on my own, in an empty apartment, never having lived alone in my life. My children were torn from me; my home was no longer mine. I hadn't worked outside my home for years and was now trying to support myself, work towards paying child support and get my feet back on solid ground.

I had only God to lean on in those dark, desperate days, but He, as always, was enough, and He began to lift me back up until I could stand; but that was going to take awhile.
A few weeks into this new phase of my life, a friend of mine introduced me to a friend of his, and we hit it off immediately. It was a surprise to me that someone would find me attractive and engaging. It was refreshing that someone was interested in talking to me for hours at a time.

I learned that Massoud was from Iran. I was just becoming familiar with people from the other side of the world, the non-Anglo side.

I grew fond of eastern music and began looking for it to listen to when I was working on my computer. I was the only white girl I knew of who actually listened to Arabic music on purpose!

In July of 2001, I was tuned in to an Arabic music chat room and quietly working on my computer at home. I'd had another child by that time and he had just turned two years old.
Being logged in to a chat room leads people to think you might want to chat, so periodically, I had little chat boxes popping up on my screen with hopeful greetings in them.

Who **Said** I Was Up For This?

The problem was, of course, that I didn't speak Arabic at all and most of the other listeners didn't speak enough English to have any kind of conversation so they were generally very brief. "Marhaba" (hello) or "Salaam al eykom" (peace be upon you) to which I would reply, "I'm sorry, I don't speak Arabic, do you speak English?" and the conversation would end there. At a time when I wasn't logged in to my usual music chat room, a little chat window popped up with a greeting in English but with a decidedly non-English name.

I responded to the greeting but when the stranger started to chat, I insisted "he" (I assumed it was a "he") tell me how he got my screen name since I knew I had not encountered this person in any chat room. He quickly apologized and offered to just leave me alone. I told him that he didn't have to leave me alone; he just had to let me know how he had found me. As a woman alone, I needed to be aware of online activities to make sure I was not at risk at all.

Finally, he told me that he was in an internet café in Gaza and the guy at the computer next to him had given him my screen name on a piece of paper and encouraged him to contact me, saying I was "nice.

I was shocked. I was "nice"? How could anyone have decided that about me and who was this other person who had recommended me?

I demanded to know the screen name of that other person who had passed along my name and recognized him as one of the non-English speakers who had tried to say hello to me the day before.

I was content with the story as it all added up to me, so I was willing to continue the conversation.

It was my first encounter with Hamoudi.

For the **Love** of Hamoudi

I had met many people online and had learned how to tell if someone was lying to you about their personal life. I had quickly learned that if a man told me that he was "separated", it usually meant that his wife was in the other room and if he told me that he was "divorced", it often mean that she wasn't home from work yet. Yes, I'd become a little cynical of meeting people online. I had learned that if I were only given a cell phone number, it was because his wife would answer the home number.

Hamoudi was like no one I had ever met before, and the best part was that I wasn't even looking! He came completely out of the blue, as if God Himself orchestrated our meeting.

We talked for a long time that first time and knew we wanted to talk again. Almost immediately, we'd exchanged phone numbers. I waited to see what he was going to give me. He gave me his cell phone number and his home phone number and his best friend's phone number. He then told me the names of all of his siblings in case any of them answered the phone at home. Yes, I was sure this one was not trying to hide anything.

Hamoudi gradually gave me a very long list of friends that I could call if I ever had trouble reaching him. He assured me that every one of them would know who I was. I loved that. He wasn't trying to hide me nor was he trying to hide anything from me. I felt secure enough to be open to seeing where this relationship might lead. I could have never guessed it would lead me down a path that would change my life forever, and bring me the love of my life.

I wonder, if I had known what this journey would bring, would I have taken this path? Would I have felt strong enough for the challenges that were to come?

Who **Said** I Was Up For This?

I'm so grateful that I had no idea what was coming!

When I learned that Hamoudi was Palestinian, I was intrigued. I'd never met a Palestinian before but I had grown up with very strong opinions about Israel.

I was curious to know what Hamoudi had to say on the subject of the whole Middle East conflict. At least we were getting off to an easy start. (NOT!)

When I asked him for his take on the situation, his answer both surprised and pleased me. He said to me, "You don't need my opinion, you need to form you own". Wow. In all my years in church, I had never heard these words. For everything I've been told in life I've never ever been told this. He wasn't going to give me his opinion on something that filled every part of his life. I was seriously impressed.

He gave me a broad variety of news and information websites, some Palestinian, some Israeli, and some European. He told me to start reading, and if there was anything I wanted to discuss, he would welcome any discussion, and if I had any questions, I should feel free to ask.

I started digging and was very surprised by the result. One site linked to another and I found myself devouring information day and night. I kept reading and reading and was surprised to find Christian sites that told a very different story that what I heard growing up.

I learned of the agony of Palestinians. I learned of their displacement as a people. Why had I never heard of this before? How could I have spent so many years being in favour of all this suffering? I was shaken to the core. As a Christian, I had believed that I was to be loving and compassionate, that my hand was to be extended to everyone, and certainly always to fellow Christians.

53

Now I was learning that my beliefs, which I had thought were Biblically based, were putting me on the side of supporting the oppression of a whole people group. How could I coincide my faith with the outcome of what I believed? I was overcome with the weight of what I had been supporting: the death and misery of a nation. This is not who I wanted to be.

It was not what I intended at all.

I had great difficulty coping with the knowledge of what I'd been supporting for so many years. It was completely opposed to the principles I believed in and followed. How could this have happened? I simply did not know.

My heart was broken before God and I prayed to be forgiven for my foolishness. There was no excuse for my ignorance. I was a grown woman and I could blame no one else for the decisions I made. I had chosen to blindly accept the teaching that Israel was right and therefore should not be questioned. Even as I see the words forming on the page I can see that this makes no sense at all.

I prayed and cried tears of repentance and regret for the agony I had allowed. So many people had suffered; so many had lost so much; so many had died. Through all of it, I had been fully accepting of the outcomes. This had to stop immediately. If I believed what I claimed to believe, then I could no longer ignorantly support such violations of God's principles, as I understood them.

For a month I prayed and cried and begged God to forgive my ignorant support of such terrible things. As that month drew to a close, I felt God's hand on me, giving me peace. I understood that if I could have supported the suffering of Palestinians in my ignorance, then now that I was fully aware, it was my responsibility to work for peace and justice.

Who **Said** I Was Up For This?

I have often felt like Neo in The Matrix, when he was offered the choice of the red or blue pills. One would keep him fully aware of the truth; the other would allow him to return to being blissfully ignorant of the facts. It can be a heavy burden to know the truth and it would be tempting to be able to "unknow". There is, however, no such option. I knew. And I had to act.

I became involved in local pro-Palestinian activities and groups, including the Canadian Palestinian Association. I attended every rally and demonstration I was able to get to and I even brought my children. I needed them to escape the ignorance that had gotten me stuck for so many years.

As I marched through the streets of Vancouver, I noticed that I was marching with Muslims, Jews, atheists, communists, feminists, gay and lesbian groups and anarchists, but I saw no group who identified themselves as Christians. This was troubling to me. Where was the Christian presence in support of Palestinians? There are Christians in Palestine who are suffering alongside their Muslim neighbours so why aren't the Christians speaking out?

I felt very much alone but more determined than ever to be that one voice, even if I am the only one.

I continued to attend the rallies and demonstrations and asked other Christians to come but they never did. Finally during the heavy Israeli assault of Operation Cast Lead from December 2008 to January 2009, I attended a demonstration with some Palestinian Christian friends as well as my parents. It was a huge victory for me to have them attend with me. In eight years it was the first time my parents came. I didn't mind. I didn't even count those years. I was just grateful that they finally came.

For the **Love** of Hamoudi

From the time I got to know Hamoudi, I began to see the hand of God at work in our relationship and it was most remarkable.

I learned that his people were largely refugees. I had lost my home and all that was familiar. God allowed me to experience a taste of what it was like to be a refugee.

Many of his people have had their homes demolished and have nowhere else to live. God allowed me to lose my home and have to sleep in my van for a while, allowing me to get a taste of what homelessness was like.

Many Palestinians have lost children, the youngest most vulnerable casualties of the violence going on around them. Although my children did not die, they were kept away from me. My heart and soul were deeply wounded and filled with sorrow and longing for them.

God allowed me to understand the heartache of such a profound loss of those who are most precious.

It was through the losses in my life that I gained an intimate understanding of Palestinians. As I began to realize that few others could truly relate, I learned to be grateful for the trials I had endured because, without them, I would never have become the person I had become; deeply compassionate and committed to the oppressed.

It was amazing to me that God had stripped me of all pretence. I had been humbled and had all of my old support system taken away. I had made mistakes, and made errors in judgment. I know that there were choices that I had made that had not contributed well to my overall situation. For years I bore a heavy burden for my mistakes. I carried shame and humiliation as my constant companions. I didn't feel deserving of more than I had been left with.

Who **Said** I Was Up For This?

My ex husband took me to court several times over custody issues. He had told the judge false stories about me in order to prejudice the court against me, and it worked. Little by little he was able to take away more of the precious time I had with my children.

As I began to learn more about the sorrow and injustice that Hamoudi's people had been enduring for so many years, I realized that I really did understand. I learned to be grateful for my own history of pain and injustice because through it, God had given me the gifts of tenderness and compassion that I probably wouldn't have had if my life had been simpler. I understood how it felt to be on the short side of injustice, to be maligned, to be unfairly characterized and constantly judged on my past.

The more I understood the needs and heartbreak of Hamoudi's nation, the more I realized that I understood only because of the difficulties that I had experienced in my own life.

I still whine about the things in my life, but I don't let it last long. I remember that it was a very important lesson to prepare me for wonderful things that were coming.

It's amazing how a little perspective can ease our own sense of suffering. I really love that.

Shortly after Hamoudi and I met online, along came September 11, 2001, a day that will be remembered for a very long time. It was the kind of day where most of us remember clearly where we were and what we were doing when we heard the news of the planes.

I'm so grateful that I met Hamoudi before this happened because I don't honestly know how the strong anti-Arab sentiment that ensued would have affected me. As it was, I already knew what kind of a man Hamoudi was and God had dealt with me regarding my attitude towards Palestinians, so I never did get caught up in the hate and fear that followed. By then, I was aware enough of the political climate as it affected Palestine that I was struck with fear for Hamoudi when I was watching the news of the World Trade Centre.

I called him and said that I didn't want to scare him, but I had serious concerns for his safety. I told him that I wanted to be wrong but I had a terrible feeling that Israel would use the distraction of the US's outrage to provide the necessary cover for them to launch a very strong attack against the Palestinians.

I was reluctant to say anything because I didn't want to cause Hamoudi any undo fear, but I felt I needed to warn him and to start praying.

The winter of 2001 into the spring of 2002 saw some of the heaviest attacks until that time. We were sure things couldn't get any worse than that. It was during this time that the Israeli army would approach a town or refugee camp and order all the men, aged 15 and up, to present themselves to be arrested. Omar, Hamoudi's younger brother, turned 15 that year and I remember being on the phone with him as the army was making its way through the Gaza Strip and approaching Gaza City.

My heart broke when he said, "Is this why I'm turning 15, Linda? So I'm old enough for them to arrest me?"

I held back my tears and tried to assure him that he would be all right. I promised to pray for him and told him that God was still in charge, even though times were so very dark and scary.

Who **Said** I Was Up For This?

When the army came to a town or refugee camp, everyone was placed under curfew. Families were starving in their own homes because they were unable to get out to buy more groceries.

In Hamoudi's household, there was his dad and step-mom, his grandma, three sisters and his brother. If they were unable to get out for more food, it wouldn't take long for their supplies to be used up.

With the economy being as bad as it is in Gaza, it's rare to have enough money to stock up on groceries so, if disaster strikes, it will hit very hard.

I had no money. In fact, I only had a part time job so for me to send Hamoudi enough money for extra groceries was out of the question, but as we watched the news and saw town after town under curfew and starving, I was desperate to make sure this didn't happen to Hamoudi and his family.

The only thing of value I owned was a vintage Coca Cola machine. My ex husband had bought it for me on my thirtieth birthday. I loved it. I had wanted one for years and was thrilled to get it. When faced with the possibility of Hamoudi's family getting caught without enough food to get them through a prolonged curfew, I didn't even have to think twice. I sold the machine immediately and sent the money to Hamoudi at once.

He was able to get out to the market and buy tons of food for his family! Their house was then well enough stocked to withstand a curfew that might last for several days. I was so relieved and kept watching the news, but now with a measure of hope that I didn't have before, and with a spirit of joyful gratitude that God had given me something of value so I was able to do something good for this family.

The horror in town after town was hard to bear, especially as I knew that Hamoudi and his family were bracing themselves for their turn. From online news sources, I learned that the Palestinian Authority was advising its police officers to take off their uniforms and put their weapons away because the army was targeting them. I saw grisly pictures of groups of police officers who had been rounded up and executed all together in a room.

Hamoudi was a police officer at the time, and this news sent shivers down my spine and turned my stomach to ice. I called him and asked him if he'd been given these instructions and he said that he hadn't heard anything. There was so much confusion and fear that I wasn't surprised that messages were not getting through.

I carefully suggested that he take this advice and go home and stay safe. His reply broke my heart as much as it made me proud of him. He told me, "Let them kill me with my uniform on. I'm not taking it off for anybody. If they want me, they can find me. I'm not hiding from anyone."

I couldn't ask him again. I just prayed as hard as I could that God would protect him and somehow stop this nightmare.

The army stopped just before it got to Gaza City. Hamoudi and his family were safe.

I learned as much about faith as I did about Palestine. I learned to pray about everything. I learned to hope for everything. I have no idea why God chose me for this. I'm a goof, a knucklehead. I like to play and have fun. I'm a terrible procrastinator. I don't have a degree in International Relations or in Middle Eastern Studies. I have nothing. I was a single mother struggling with court and being under employed and sorting out custody and access issues. There was nothing about me that would suggest that I was the right person to be involved with someone from Gaza to the point that I was involved. But there I was, and wouldn't you know it? I was exactly the right person for the job! God, Himself, had orchestrated the events in my life to create in me the right heart and spirit to reach out in love and to endure the agony that this love would bring.

In March 2002, I wrote an article based on a conversation I was having with someone regarding suicide bombers. It was published online:

> *Someone asked me . . .*
> *by Linda Todd*
>
> *Someone asked me what I was doing to discourage suicide bombers. I wrote this reply:*
>
> *I think that raising awareness and understanding is one of the keys to finding a way to a solution; or at least making some positive alterations to the current situation.*
>
> *Before I answer your question, I think it is important to first ask and answer another question: What is it that is encouraging these bombers? If I am to know how to discourage them, then first I have to know what is encouraging them so I can combat it.*
>
> *The general answer, from which I will also bring out specifics, is that it is the ongoing inhumane illegal occupation of the Palestinian people by the Israeli government and carried out by the brutal Israeli army.*

Let's understand what this means:

It means that children never know which days they will be allowed to go to school. More than that, they don't even know if their school will still be standing.
If they are going to school, they are too often abused, assaulted and terrorized by Israeli settlers and their children as well as Israeli soldiers.

Living under this occupation also means never knowing when you'll be able to go to the market to replenish your household supplies and when you hear the announcement that you are now allowed to go, just as you venture far enough from home to be out of range of any protective cover, another announcement is heard saying that the previous announcement is no longer in effect; and then the soldiers start shooting at all the people "violating curfew". You run out of the store when you hear the shooting and find that your daughter who was waiting for you in the car has been virtually decapitated by the number of bullet holes across her neck. It's not the last memory of your 6yr old that you were hoping for.

You stagger home, stunned and dazed and try to think of how you will tell your wife and children why you are coming home alone when you see on the news that the Israeli government has been gently chided for using excessive force while being patted on the back for taking a stand against terrorism and in defense of their security.

You slump into your chair and ask yourself what kind of a threat your little girl had been and how did it make the Israelis feel safer to terrorize a community of hungry families trying to buy some food.

Living under occupation also means knowing that 80% of the country's water supply is given to the Israelis while only 20% is allotted for Palestinians (http://www. palestinemonitor.org/factsheet/water_inequalities.htm) What does this mean? It means that you may or may not have enough water to drink, bathe, cook, wash while looking out across the road and seeing communities with big swimming pools and sprinklers on everyday.

When you are lucky enough to have the water turned on in your area, there may not be enough pressure to fill the water tank which is on your roof - that is, if it hasn't been shot off yet. Water tanks have been a favourite target of Israeli snipers.

Living under occupation means celebrating your 15th birthday with family and friends just in time to hear on the news that the Israeli army is coming to your neighbourhood to arrest ALL males aged 15 and up. You watch helplessly as your mother bursts into tears. Your younger brother was shot in the head and killed a few months ago because he was throwing stones at the tanks that came blasting into your street, and now she is afraid she will lose another son.

Living under occupation means that as you and your wife are rushing to the hospital because she is in labour, you get held up at a check point. Your brother, who accompanied you to the hospital, gets out of the car to explain the urgency of your situation to the soldiers and when he is done, they shoot him and walk away. Your wife gives birth in the back of the car and then she slowly bleeds to death while you wait for permission to move ahead. By the time you are allowed to pass through to the hospital, your baby has also passed away.

Living under occupation also means getting a call from your buddy while you're at work. He takes you to a nearby cafe because your fiancé is trying to call from overseas. You talk and laugh for a few precious moments and as you are returning to work, you hear heavy gunfire and see huge black Apache death ships hanging in the air firing missiles into the building you had just come out of. You catch your breath and thank God that He urged your mate to call you when she did.

Occupation means that when numbers of injured lying in the streets, bleeding and screaming for help are getting higher and higher, there are no ambulances allowed in. They are shot at if they try. Eventually the cries and groans and screams are silenced as the injured become more of the dead.

There is no "combat zone" because the nightmare is all around you. There is no safe place to hide.

You keep your family in your home and suddenly there is a loud knock at the door.

The soldiers come in and force all of you to squeeze into one room. You can hear them scuffling all around your house but you can't see what they are doing. Then your home is rocked by a deafening explosion - your children scream as you and your wife try to protect them. When you can finally assess the damage, you see that the soldiers have blown up your kitchen and bathroom. Your children look at you and ask "WHY???" through their tears.
Their home has been reduced to a shell - and you know you are one of they lucky ones, because you just heard about your neighbour whose home collapsed on their whole family when the soldiers blew up a nearby home.

Your shock turns to horror when you learn that your

neighbour's wife, who was due to give birth this week, was hit by the falling debris. She was injured, but when rescuers tried to get at her, the soldiers wouldn't let them. She bled to death in the night and her soon to be born infant died with her.

Her children are in shock, and can only mumble - WHY?

You attend peaceful demonstrations, you write letters to other government leaders.

You help reporters come in and observe all that has been happening to you in hopes that the people of the world will step in and somehow bring about an end to this living hell you are caught in.

You hear rumours of peace but then the shooting starts again.

Your son is growing into a man so quickly that you hardly notice. Then you realize it's because he never really got a chance to be a child. In his young life, he saw his brother murdered because he threw stones, he saw his father humiliated again and again by soldiers barely old enough to be on duty. He has mourned the senseless death of his mother and new brother or sister - he'll never know now. He has watched his people cry out to the world for decades and no one has come to protect him.

He doesn't believe that there is another life, because this refugee camp is all he has ever known.

He's never tasted freedom; never known what it was to be able to dream and make goals for himself. He has seen what happens to people who dare to speak out because their photos adorn the walls of the ghetto he calls home. There is a special wall for the photos of the children who have been murdered and he walks past it everyday.

This boy doesn't know any families at all who have not lost a loved one to the occupation.

One day he wakes up and realizes that he is already dead. He may still be breathing, but he has no life but this hell surrounding him. He has no illusions of going to college or university because the soldiers have closed all schools and even bombed the university. Even if it were still usable, they have passed a new rule that doesn't allow him to travel.

The enemy has the power to come into his town, onto his street and into his own home anytime they want. They never have to ask; they take what they want, kill whomever they choose, and walk away without any explanations or apologies.

He knows that it is only a matter of time until he feels the hot sting of a bullet tearing through him. He has often wondered what his brother was thinking as the bullets tore through him.

He doesn't know anything about diplomacy, or what makes a good tactical decision.

He only knows that he will not allow himself to pass from this life without taking a stand for his people, for his mother, her baby, his brother, his little sisters, whose eyes never lose the look of sadness and fear, and his father who suffers shame and humiliation because he is unable to work and provide for his family because he is no longer allowed to enter the region where his job is. He used to raise vegetables on a small plot of land until the soldiers came and plowed it under and then claimed the land as their own.

This sad, angry young man has seen more sorrow in his short life than most of us will ever imagine in a hundred years; and on that day, he decides he has seen enough to know that he is the only one who can do anything about it.

Since he already considers himself to be dead, he has nothing to lose. In his mind, this is the way to win back the dignity which was stolen from him and his family.
In his mind, he is going to attack the enemy with the only weapon he has, his own body, thereby making a chance that his sisters and his father will at least have something to be proud of.

Should we be shocked that he no longer sees the enemy as people who just are going about their lives? No; not at all!

This boy and his people have never had a chance even to know what it means to just go about their business.
He walks into the crowded mall. As he looks around, he sees people laughing and talking, eating and drinking.
They don't care that his neighbours are all starving. They don't care that his family has mourned the loss of 3 precious members already this year. They are laughing; and he feels like they are laughing at him, at his suffering, at his pain.

He knows that many of these people are the same ones who ride into his community and leave death and destruction in their wake.

Of course, unlike them, he won't be home for dinner tonight.

What am I doing to discourage these bombers? I am currently trying to arrange support for the children of Mrs. Noha Sabri Swidan who just yesterday suffered the loss of their mother and their unborn brother or sister. I want these children to be comforted with the thought that their mother did not die for nothing. I want them to know that her death caused tremors half a world away.

If I can effectively convince these children that they ARE cared for and that someone IS trying to help them, then I have a chance to plant seeds of HOPE in their hearts which the Israeli Occupation Forces are working so hard to destroy; and in doing so, can save these children from becoming the next wave of human bombs.

Chapter Five

A very long eight years

If someone had told me that I would fall in love with this man almost immediately but not be able to be with him for eight years, I'm not so sure I would have been up for it. Thank goodness we don't always get to know the whole plan from the beginning!

After that first terrible winter and spring I was getting a very good idea of what I was in for, and yet, it was much too late to walk away.

I could have never guessed how God was going to use me to save Hamoudi's life, and how many times. I don't understand why He needed me, except that He knew that Hamoudi and I needed each other and so He chose me to be part of keeping Hamoudi alive and not simply loving him.

After the Israeli army miraculously came to a stop, practically at his doorstep, Hamoudi started making sure he asked me to pray for him all the time. Even he could see there was something going on here that neither of us could fully explain. It wasn't always military attacks that put Hamoudi at risk. Sometimes it was something much more mundane.

I called Hamoudi at work one day and he didn't sound like his usual, energetic self. He sounded like he wasn't feeling well at all. When I asked him if he was all right, he responded by asking me, "What does it mean if I'm yellow?"

I was completely thrown off by the question. I thought maybe he had heard this expression and wanted to know what it meant. It couldn't be that he was asking about what it meant if he was literally the colour yellow. That didn't make any sense.

So I asked him what he was talking about.

"You know, if you're yellow; if your skin is yellow, if your eyes are yellow. You know, if you're yellow. What does that mean?" I panicked. I lost all touch with everything I knew about various illnesses and all I knew is that he was really sick! I tried to answer his questions but had to keep reminding myself to breathe in order to do so.

"It's a problem with . . . with . . . with . . . " I couldn't remember! I knew this one but in my panic over Hamoudi's state of health, I could not remember the name of his liver or the name of the disease of hepatitis.

"It's a problem with your stomach – sort of", I managed to finally say.

"My stomach? You mean like I ate something bad?" he asked, sounding a little confused.

Oh dear. That wasn't it. How could I tell him what was wrong when I was in too much of a panic to remember any words that would be useful for him?

I kept trying to think, to remember what it was called. No luck.

"No no, baby, it's in your liver, (I finally remembered!) and you need to see a doctor right away!"

A Very **Long** Eight Years

It was obvious that he was very sick as I could hear him getting more sluggish even in the length of time we'd been talking.

He kept asking me what was wrong with him and, no matter how hard I tried, I could not remember the name of the disease, but I did know it was very serious.

"You have to go to the hospital now. Go NOW! Please, stop whatever you're doing and just go now," I begged him.

His illness was starting to get the better of him and he was having difficulty understanding my urgency.

"Just let me call my family. I need to talk to my boss and see if I can go." I obviously wasn't making myself clear. From the sound of his voice, I knew I had to get through to him quickly. "No baby, you need to go now. You need to TELL your boss you're leaving and go to the hospital. Tell your family to meet you there. Please don't wait – go NOW.

Hamoudi continued to ramble on about who he would call and whether he would go to the hospital or just to the doctor. Finally, in a desperate attempt to get him to the help he needed, I said clearly and calmly, "Baby, hang up right now. Stop talking to me and get yourself to the hospital NOW. Don't call anyone else until you are at the hospital. You need to go NOW.

Finally, he agreed to go and hung up, telling me to call him at the office a little later when he'd return. Of course, he wouldn't be back at work that day.

As soon as he walked into the hospital, he was taken to a bed and immediately admitted. His hepatitis was very bad by that time so, he needed urgent care.

For the **Love** of Hamoudi

Hamoudi spent over two weeks in the hospital recovering. During this time I did a lot of research on hepatitis in an effort to help him regain and then maintain his health. He was concerned that I would believe that hepatitis is exclusively a sexually transmitted disease, as many around him believed. It was very important to him that I knew he had not been unfaithful to me.

At first, it was simply a choice I made to believe and trust him, but as I did more research on this disease, and its widespread presence in Gaza, I came to realize that this disease was very common and easily transmitted and, in fact, was least often transmitted through sexual contact.

Although Hamoudi and I lived on opposite sides of the world and we had never been able to touch each other, we still valued the exclusivity of our relationship. Although there were a few times when we broke up briefly due to the overwhelming stress of such a relationship, we always came back to a deep committed love that had the highest regard for each other.

The times when we did break up, it was most often due to my own insecurities. I had been through a very difficult marriage and divorce. It had ravaged my self-esteem and left me believing that I was very forgettable. With Hamoudi and I being so far apart, I had a very hard time believing that he could actually love me and want me and not be pursuing other women. What was special about me that I should be able to keep his attention? I never had an answer to that question.

Hamoudi always told me he loved me but the fact that we had never been together, geographically, made it easy for me to convince myself that, as had happened to me in the past, it was only a matter of time until he changed his mind, or found a prettier, thinner, younger woman and I would be

72

out of his life anyways. I am several years older than he and I have children; huge challenges on their own for any man. Add to that the distance, and my deep insecurities, and periodically, it just became too much for me to believe and I would break up with him. I would tell my self that it was for his own good. I would tell myself that it would be better for him to find a woman who was close by, who he could marry without delay. Each time, however, I tried to let him go, I dreaded the thought of him meeting any other woman.

I would tell myself that I couldn't handle a long distance relationship with no clear end date. How long could we go on like this? Year after year would pass and we were no closer to being together. I was getting pressured by some of my friends to forget about him. They would tell me that I couldn't trust him; he's just using me.

We lived in such different worlds, and in my world, I was the only one who knew him. My own fears plus the pressures of well-meaning friends would bring me to the conclusion that I needed to try to let him go.

I can't ever forget the agony in his voice. Hamoudi has one of the most beautiful, vibrant voices I know. He is filled with enthusiasm and life but when he would get that call and I was, again, telling him I was letting him go, it was as if a black hole sucked every speck of life and light out of him.
It's painful for me to think about and I wish I could go back and be stronger, be more confident. I wish I could go back and take back every bit of pain I caused him, but I can't. I can just go forward in gratitude that God gave Hamoudi the grace and love to keep pursuing me, no matter how long I wandered from him.

Hamoudi would continue to email me, gently telling me he loved me. Letting me know how he was and checking on how I was doing without being pushy. He knew I would retreat if he tried to hard, but he couldn't stay away. He lovingly, gently drew me back to him.

April 24, 2007

Hey Princess ,
its been a while now that i havent heard from you, im just worried , is everything ok ? are you ok baby ?
its tuesday here , im at the office and i have tons of work to do , im really getting everything sorted out , i just need to know that you are ok , how are the kids ? i hope everything is fine.

as i told you in my previous email i will be getting my computer back by the end of this week , and soon after that i will get the internet connection hooked back on, this way i can keep in touch on a daily basis so i know whats going on in your world !
please try to send me an email or call me or anything , just to know that you are ok , you're still in my heart you know and nothing will ever change that , i just hope you are ok and everything is working for you.

ill be getting my wages early next month so i will call you as soon as that happens , please be safe and take good care of your self and health , i need you to stick around for a long time you know !

All my love and hugs and kisses,
Hamoudi

It was amazing to us both how it seemed that I always called him at the right time to help when he was sick or in potential danger. There was one time, however, when this was furthest from the way it worked out.

A Very **Long** Eight Years

We were talking on the phone one evening, and he was in an area where the cell phone reception was very weak. Very frequently, Israeli drones fly overhead for hours at a time and interfere with all radio and cell phone signals.

Our call was cut off, but we were in the middle of our conversation. Not to be deterred by the military activity over his head, Hamoudi got in a car to drive elsewhere to find a better signal.
I tried to call back but couldn't reach him. I kept trying and finally, a couple of hours later, I found him.

Hamoudi was in the hospital getting a bullet wound in his leg dressed. As he was on his way to find a better signal, he was stopped at a checkpoint. It was manned by Palestinian Authority policemen who knew him, so they paused to exchange pleasantries. Somehow, which was never made clear to me, this policeman accidentally fired his gun. The bullet went through the car door and into Hamoudi's leg.

The young policeman was very distraught because he would be in a lot of trouble if this incident was ever reported to headquarters. By this time, Hamoudi was an officer, and there would be serious consequences for shooting an officer, accidentally or otherwise.

Realizing that this was every bit as much a surprise to the policeman as it was to him, Hamoudi assured the young man that this incident would never be reported and he quietly took himself to the local hospital for treatment.

I guess gunshot wounds are common enough in Gaza that there is no special reporting required when a victim shows up for treatment.

Hamoudi's leg healed, and years later, when I finally got to

Gaza, he showed me the scar from his bullet wound.

There were other times, however, when it was obvious that God was using me to intercept in Hamoudi's life in a miraculous, life saving way.

Our spirits were intertwined in such a way that they seemed to know the right moment that we needed to reach out for each other.

It was common for me to try to call Hamoudi and not to be able to get through. Normally when this happened, I would simply try later, rarely using the list of friends' phone numbers that Hamoudi had given me shortly after we met and had kept updated for me. Occasionally, however, there would come a time when I just had a nagging feeling that I simply must reach him, even if I may not know why.

This was one of those times.

After several unsuccessful attempts to get through, I called Hamoudi's best friend, Ouf. As soon as I explained my problem, Ouf asked me to call back in about twenty minutes, and that he would drive to the police station where Hamoudi's office was.

I watched the minutes tick past and called again, eagerly anticipating being able to finally talk to Hamoudi. Instead, Ouf apologized and asked if I would please give him another 15 minutes. He explained that he was being delayed by the many checkpoints along the road.

I had to try a couple of more times and finally Ouf said, very apologetically, "I have him in the car now. Just give us five minutes and I'll take him to a café so you can talk."

A Very **Long** Eight Years

By this time, almost an hour and a half had passed for a trip that was expected to take less than twenty minutes, so frequent were the military check points all through Gaza, both Israeli and Palestinian.

When I called back, Hamoudi finally answered the phone! By this time, I felt silly for putting Ouf through so much for us to talk. Hamoudi and I had a few wonderful minutes of relaxed conversation. I explained that I honestly didn't know why it was so important that I reach him. I just had a feeling that something was up and I needed to hear his voice.

He reassured me that all was well. He was just at the Naval Police headquarters, located down at the beach, on the shore of the Mediterranean Sea. I told him how lucky he was to be stationed in such an exotic location, even though from where he sat, there was very little that felt exotic about it.

We couldn't talk for too long because he had to get back to work. We both thought it was funny that so much effort had gone into setting up a few minutes of casual conversation. I was convinced that I could calm down and stop worrying about him.

We hung up and Ouf drove Hamoudi back to work.

The next day, when Hamoudi and I spoke, he told me a story that shook me to the core.

After we hung up, he and Ouf left the café and began the drive back to the beach headquarters. They were on the road that ran parallel to the beach and as they approached their turn, they could hear the sound of heavy guns firing, but couldn't see what the source of the noise was.

When they turned the corner to approach Hamoudi's workplace, the sight caught them both off guard. Hovering in the air above the Police Headquarters were two Apache helicopters, guns blasting shells into the building.

Hamoudi and Ouf were shocked, especially when they realized that were it not for my persistent phone call, Hamoudi would have been in the building when it was so violently attacked. As I heard this story, my heart was pounding and tears filled my eyes. Why did I keep calling? How could I have made Ouf go through so much trouble to get Hamoudi when I didn't even have anything important to say? Why wasn't I content to just try calling him later, like I usually did?

The answer to all of this was clear. God had once again used me to spare Hamoudi's life. We both came to that conclusion and it left us speechless. Who were we that God should intervene in our lives this way?

We quickly realized that we didn't have to know why; we just needed to be grateful that He did.

Hamoudi and I found, over the years, that when we felt that inner voice urging us to contact each other, we really needed to listen.

After the Israeli military destroyed Gaza's ability to have a naval police force, Hamoudi was moved inland to take a position with the regular police force.

His job, in the early days, was to man the checkpoints and he was most often assigned to night duty.

Nights in a Gazan winter are far from warm. The ocean breezes blow, bringing in cold, damp air that chills you to the bone.

He would stand out on the side of the road, night after night, in his police-issue long johns under his uniform and his

A Very **Long** Eight Years

overcoat on top and still he was he frozen to the bone.

I wanted to run to him with a steaming bowl of chicken soup and a big mug of hot chocolate, but since I was still a bit too far away for that, I tried to find other ways to keep him warm. As I was searching online one day, I found a site that would let me send an unlimited number of free text messages! What a gift!!

When I knew he was spending a long cold night outside, I would send him long stories, one text message at a time. I would send him romantic tales of our future or adventure stories or whatever I could think of in the moment. But I would write!

Hamoudi found himself eagerly looking for the next installment of my crazy stories as I helped him to pass the time. His job really didn't require any actual policing on these checkpoint nights; it was more a case of simply identifying who was driving around at night.

My stories gave him a welcome respite from the long hours of boredom. It was a small thing, but it was another one of those many moments that we found a way to deepen the bonds between us.

Sometimes, God just went ahead and spared Hamoudi's life without letting me in on it until after it was all over.
As an officer, he was the senior man on any patrols that went out to watch over the outskirts of Gaza at night. He always seemed to be working at night. That suited us because with the time difference, it allowed us both to be awake at the same time.

On one particular night, when Hamoudi was leading a patrol in the outer edges of Gaza where the city ends and there are just fields and grass, I called him as I always called him.

For the **Love** of Hamoudi

In the background I could hear the sound of voices but they sounded like they were talking to a baby. I was curious to know what was happening. How could policemen on an all night patrol be talking to a baby?

Hamoudi laughed when he told me that the 4 guys who were with him had found a baby rabbit in the grass and they were playing with it. Suddenly, the image that explanation gave me made me stop in my tracks. We always have this idea of Palestinians as being tough, perhaps mean and often, terrorists. That day, as I listened to those men's voices talking in that high, sweet way that people use when they're talking to a baby was such a contrast to what we typically think of as what a Palestinian is like.

I listened to them in the background for the whole time I talked to Hamoudi. By the time we hung up, I was so happy and felt warm with the knowledge that Hamoudi was with such a great bunch of guys. I didn't have to worry about him on this patrol. Nothing ever happened out in the fields on the outskirts of town.

When I tried to reach him the next night, I wasn't able to, so I had to wait until the following day, and then I tried his home phone instead of his cell phone.

His older sister, Dina, answered the phone and, when I asked if I could speak to Hamoudi, her reply left me very worried. She said, "Linda, I'll let you talk to him but please don't blame him if he's rude to you. Something terrible happened, and he is feeling very bad.

My breath was stuck in my chest. What had happened? How terrible was it?

I didn't want to ask Dina. I thought that if she had wanted to tell me, she would have. I quickly assured her that I would not hold anything against Hamoudi and I would be very careful with him.

She took the phone to Hamoudi's room and passed it to him, letting him know I was on the line.

When Hamoudi took the phone, his voice sounded thick and there was a deep heaviness to it that broke my heart, even before I knew why.

The four young men he had been on patrol with when I heard them playing with the bunny had been sent out to the same location to be on patrol again the next night. Hamoudi had been sent with them but sometime during the night, he was needed back at the office so he was ordered to allow the other four men to continue their patrol without him. It was an uneventful location anyways.

When the morning patrol team finally went out to replace the four who had been out all night, they made a grisly discovery. Sometime in the night, an Israeli military plane had flown over and shot the four police officers killing some and seriously injuring others. Because of the distance from town, no one knew the men had been shot so the ones who had been injured bled to death so the morning team found the four bodies lying in the field.

As Hamoudi told me his horrifying tale, I kept hearing their voices as they played with the baby rabbit. One night before they died, they had been so happy; four young men excited with their discovery that made their mundane job suddenly enjoyable.

My heart was breaking for them and their families. These four young men had done nothing wrong. In fact, they were on patrol to make sure no one else did anything wrong either.

For the **Love** of Hamoudi

They had been so full of life when I had heard them, and now, for no reason at all, they were all dead.

Hamoudi was tormented with the thought that he had started the night with them but was unexpectedly called away. He was suffering from severe survivors' guilt.

"I should have been with them," he lamented. "Why did I get called away? Why did they die and not me?"

I had no answers for him. I had no wise words of comfort to say in this moment that would somehow make the senseless loss of four good young men bearable.

He was right. It wasn't fair. He was supposed to there with them and he wasn't. And now they were dead and he wasn't. There was nothing fair about it.

I desperately wanted to say something to ease his pain but I couldn't think of anything.

"I know there's nothing I can say to make any sense of why this happened to them. You're right. It's not fair, and I wish it had never happened. I am so sorry, baby. I'm so sorry. All I can say about it is that for whatever reason you were spared, I'm so grateful. I prayed for you as I always do. I don't know why God chose to spare your life, and I can't even try to comment on why they weren't spared, but I'm grateful for you"

I felt awkward and helpless, but at the same time, gratitude rose like a tidal wave from the very depths of my soul until it washed over me. He was alive. In the terrible sadness of the loss of the other four, my Hamoudi was alive. It was another example of this contrast that is Gaza. There is so much sorrow and so much joy all rolled into one place.

A Very **Long** Eight Years

After we hung up, I sat in stunned silence, barely able to breathe, and then my tears found their way out and couldn't be stopped. I wept, alone in my room. There were tears of relief and tears of overwhelming sadness. Yes, my beloved was alive, but he was so wounded by the shocking way he lost his four friends.

I longed to put my arms around him and take away his pain but I was stuck on the opposite side of the world.

Once again, in that violent, cruel land, God had reached His hand into Hamoudi's life and saved him from certain death. I had never seen prayer work like this. I had heard stories but had never seen it for myself. It's as humbling as it is exciting. I began to take prayer very seriously. It became so Hamoudi's name was always on my lips, being lifted in prayer as I did whatever it was I was doing at the time.

I didn't dare not pray for him. Although I couldn't explain it, I knew that God had joined us together in a way I'd never experienced before, but must not take lightly. Hamoudi and I were meant to be. God was using me to keep him alive.

It felt like loving Hamoudi was a direct order from Heaven and I dare not turn my back. This proved to be true even at the times I broke up with him. No matter what happened, we were always drawn back to each other. No one could ever fill the place we had only for each other.

Articles about Hamoudi and me

> *GAZA, June 5 (Xinhua) – For Hamoudi Gharib, time ticked too slowly on a June day as he was waiting for his Canadian would-be wife to cross into the besiege Gaza, nearly eight years after they first met over the internet.*

For the **Love** of Hamoudi

He strolled back and forth at the Gaza border, hard to cover up the longing and strain that hit him when he was about to meet his fiancée, Linda Todd, who took the adventure into Gaza by joining a group of international campaigners on a lifesaving mission.

"It was overwhelming; I can't describe it," the Gaza journalist said about his feeling at that moment. "I was happy and nervous all at the same time. I was feeling my destiny was three seconds away."

"My dream was becoming more and more real as the bus approached," he added.

Finally, the bus appeared driving from the Egyptian side and the once very active Hamoudi froze in his place, looking at the activists stepping out one by one.

When he saw Linda, he rushed and hugged her with the eyes of Hamas security men gazing in wonder.

Her colleagues applauded and cheered joyfully before the pressmen turned their cameras to Hamoudi and let his story hit the headlines, predominating over the news of the pro-Palestinian delegation that came in solidarity with the Gaza Strip.

Hamoudi's story goes back to the year of 2001 when the couple met on the Internet and started chatting on-line for several hours each day, trying to know more about each other's worlds which were quite different.

"I loved that person for caring so much about me," Hamoudi said, speaking about how an ordinary chat conversation developed into a love story. "Two nights after we met, she called me and we talked over the phone for hours," he recalled.

A Very **Long** Eight Years

Being a Gaza resident, it means traveling out from Gaza requires clearance from Israel, the Palestinian National Authority (PNA), Egypt, and finally Hamas, the Islamic movement that seized control of the coastal enclave in the summer of 2007.

And for Linda, entering Gaza was not easy either.

"Every time we would think that maybe this time we got together either there was something wrong on my side, or suddenly the borders were closed, or suddenly there was something going on like too much violence," the new bride said in an interview at her husband's family house.

Linda joined an international delegation called Code Pink, which, after four months of preparations, decided to visit Gaza after Israel ended its three-week major military offensive against the blockaded coastal territory in January.

The peace mission was miraculously permitted to enter Gaza through Rafah crossing on the border with Egypt.

Linda's friends said seeing the two united and married made them forget all the hard times they experienced during their trip, especially the three-day waiting in Egypt.

The newlyweds are now happily living together in Gaza spending their honeymoon in the Gaza City that has been experiencing the most tragic and unprecedented ordeal in its history.

"Patience had been the biggest lesson," Linda said.

But the happy life the two are living now is mixed with

worry about separation. Linda, who took a vacation from her work, has to go back to Canada, and Hamoudi will "most probably try to follow her," she said.

Since Gaza blockade has been tightened by time, Hamoudi is afraid it will take him years to rejoin with his wife, but the couple is determined to overcome the siege. "We promised each other not to give in under any circumstance."

Travel restriction on the Gazans was first applied at the beginning of the Palestinian intifada (uprising) in 2000. But it started to take the toll on the public in 2006 when Hamas captured an Israeli soldier in a cross-border raid near Gaza.

Israel ended its occupation of Gaza in 2005 and withdrew from settlements, handing it over to native Palestinians. In June 2007, Hamas militants, who reject peace with Israel, wrested control of the territory from the Fatah group which is seeking a peace deal with the Jewish state.

As a result, Egypt and Israel maintained a full closure of their borders with the Hamas-controlled Gaza Strip.

Egypt opens Rafah crossing point, Gaza's only gateway bypassing Israel to the outside world, for humanitarian cases for two days per month. Hundreds of Gazans have died due to the siege over the past couple of years.

Prospects of lifting the Israeli embargo hinge on healing the Palestinian split between Hamas and President Mahmoud Abbas' Fatah party, but so far talks towards this goal have made no substantial progress.

Egypt said it would open Rafah crossing regularly if the Palestinian groups reconciled through a Cairo-hosted dialogue, but recent gun battles in the West Bank between Hamas and Palestinian security forces loyal to Abbas fueled speculations that the dialogue was not going to succeed.

Romance Blooms, Even in Gaza – May 30, 2010
By Pam Bailey

Today we almost literally "sailed" into Gaza. I say, "sailed", because it was incredibly easy this time. We seemed to have pushed all the right buttons...with the Egyptian Embassy, State Department and Congressmen back home, and the Egyptian Embassy and Intelligence Service in Cairo. But I say "almost" because the two young Egyptian women – one an artist who works with children and another who is a media coordinator in Alexandria's Department of Culture – who had tried to travel in with us were turned away as a "security" risk. We delayed the entry of the rest of the group for three hours trying to get them in . . . to no avail.

Our arrival in Gaza had a special joyousness to it for another reason as well: One of our delegates – Linda Todd of British Columbia – revealed the night before that upon crossing into Gaza, she planned to marry Hamoudi Gharib, a local correspondent for the Xinhua News Agency in China. Linda – an administrative assistant for the Canadian federal government and a mother of five – had "met" him online eight years ago when she frequented a chat room that featured Arabic music as background (and thus made for a good "companion" while she worked on other projects). When she was asked by men if she wanted to be "friends," she would politely respond by explaining that she didn't speak Arabic, rather than just ignore them. One of her "rejected" would-be friends passed her name to a companion who spoke English, saying she sounded like a nice woman. The rest is history. For eight years, she and Hamoudi chatted by web cam and in April, now engaged, she jumped at the chance to join the May/June CODEPINK delegation to Gaza.

Once she leaked her secret, we couldn't help but get involved. We accompanied her in Al Arish, the last town before the Gazan border, to purchase a beautiful Palestinian dress and scarf. When we finally rolled through the Rafah crossing, she found a restroom and transformed from ordinary mom to "Super Goddess."

I only wish we had been able to capture in a bottle the look of sheer happiness (and relief) that shone through when the two were united for the first time. What more fitting way to show one's support for and faith in the people of Gaza? A wedding implies a future, after all

Chapter Six

I'm Stuck on You

The years seemed to roll endlessly on. Each year brought the same distance, and never enough money to do anything about it. I couldn't let go of the belief that Hamoudi and I would be together one day, but I just couldn't see how it was going to happen. He was closed in; I was closed out; there just seemed to be no way to end our agony.

When Hamoudi called me in December of 2008 to give me the news that they were under attack, I ran to my computer and started scanning for news of Gaza and found, to my horror, that Israel had just begun a major offensive action they called "Operation Cast Lead". There were bombs falling all over Gaza. In all the years I'd witnessed the suffering there, I had never seen an attack of this magnitude.

I wanted to scream and cry, but I would have to breathe in order to do that and my breath was stuck in my chest. My tears silently poured down my cheeks as I read through different websites, all showing the same ghastly pictures of destruction.

After all these years and all of our trials, I just couldn't accept that it was going to end like this. I simply could not believe that everything we had gone through was so I could watch his death on the evening news.

I called Hamoudi at the end of each of his days. I needed to know he was still alive. As his days closed, mine were just

For the **Love** of Hamoudi

beginning and I began each day with all the latest news of the war on Gaza.

Hamoudi had begun working for a news agency as the attack started and, as their reporter, he had to walk through the streets and the hospitals and document those who were killed or injured. It was so far beyond a nightmare for him that I am at a loss of words to describe his experience.

For me, they were some of the most difficult days in my life. I would hang up the phone each day and cry and pray that God would somehow protect Hamoudi's mind from the agony he was forced to live through everyday.

I finally came to the point where I didn't feel that I could hear anymore. I live in Canada. War is completely foreign to anything that I've ever been familiar with and hearing each detail of what Hamoudi was seeing in Gaza was getting to be too much for me.

However, every time I would think that I couldn't take any more, I would think of what my Hamoudi was going through and I realized that he needed so much more support than I did and I would take a deep breath and call him again.
It was surreal to hang up the phone and head off to work where everyone was just living his or her lives. For me, there was no more "normal"; for me, everyday I was immersed in the attack on Gaza.

One of the times I called, I heard a BOOM in the background and Hamoudi quickly said, "My building's been hit; I have to go NOW!"

The line went dead and I sat in stunned silence, shaking, not knowing what happened, not knowing if my Hamoudi had survived the hit.

I Am **Stuck** on You

I called back later, hoping he would answer his phone. He did! He had been in a building that was full of press agencies. It wasn't supposed to be hit but it was and the hit sent all the journalists, cameramen and other staff into the street. His family had heard of the hit and quickly turned on their TV to see if there was any news on the event. They didn't know if Hamoudi was dead or alive until they saw him on their screen! One of the cameramen took footage of the entire group of journalists rushing out of the building and Hamoudi was one of them. He was working for Press TV at the time, and so as soon as he hit the ground he began reporting on the situation while he was hoping to avoid any further air strikes.

I don't know how he survived that attack. It was the worst invasion that Gaza has known in my experience. I'm just grateful that God gave me the strength to listen to whatever Hamoudi had to say. Together, we limped through those 23 days, clinging to each other in very dark times.

After the fire

I don't remember how we made it through that attack without completely losing our minds. Somewhere in the middle of all of that madness, I realized that I simply could not imagine life without him. It seemed that if we didn't find a way to get married now, it would be too late. I knew that I couldn't live without my Hamoudi.

He had asked me to marry him so many times over the years and I had told him, "Yes", but then I wasn't sure. Now I was sure. I had never before been faced with such a very real possibility of him not surviving. The thought of losing him was simply unbearable. There was no more uncertainty, no more doubts. We needed to get together and get married and do whatever it took to live happily ever after.

I started asking everyone that I knew who was involved in Palestinian matters how I could get to Gaza. I knew enough to know that it was somewhere between extremely difficult and impossible to get there. I needed a good strategy.

I knew that someone would have the answer I was looking for so I sent out messages and emails until the answers started coming in. Code Pink.

I had read about Code Pink months earlier but didn't know anything about them but everyone I asked sent me the same answer. I looked them up online and learned that they were planning a visit to Gaza the following June (2009), so I told them I wanted to go!

I was welcomed into the group and worked on getting the funds I needed to make the trip. My parents helped tremendously. My children all understood my many reasons for going and supported my participation in this delegation. They also supported my marrying Hamoudi. Yes, I do have the best kids in the world. By the summer of 2009, Hamoudi and I had known each other for so long and I had kept my children informed all along the way.

He was already part of the family.

I had never traveled outside North America before, so I thought it was perfect that my first big trip was to Gaza! We flew first to Cairo and met with the other delegation members before making the long bus ride to the Rafah border that is the crossing between Egypt and the Gaza Strip.

In the Cairo hotel, I was surprised to see Dr. Norman Finkelstein in our group. He is a very outspoken academic who passionately presents the case of Palestinians to audiences everywhere. I had read so much about him and was honoured to finally meet this amazing man. In person, he is gentle and soft-spoken, warm and friendly. In his writing, he is direct and fiery. I was pleasantly surprised to find how approachable and humble he is. I told him my story, and immediately had his support.

The next morning, we all boarded our travel buses and slowly rolled out of Cairo. I was so excited! We were finally on the last leg of our very long journey. For me, this was an eight-year journey. I could hardly contain my enthusiasm. Hamoudi had survived so much and I was about to finally be there with him. We were escorted by armed Egyptian security all the way from Cairo, down the long, long highway, through the Sinai Desert, up the Sinai Peninsula, to the Rafah border. I didn't find it comforting at all. I found it kind of scary to look around and see automatic weapons in the vehicles all around us. Not only that, but there were towers all along the highway, each with an armed soldier in it. Coming from Canada, I had never seen such thing. The presence of so many weapons, and people ready to use them, was as much a curiosity as it was unnerving. I couldn't tell if they were there to protect us or to shoot us.

Every new experience is something to be excited about; even if those new experiences scared me a little.

Finally, our group arrived in the small town of Al Arish, close to the border of Egypt and Gaza. Hamoudi was waiting on the other side.

For the **Love** of Hamoudi

Chapter Seven

And Back Again....

Leaving Hamoudi behind at the border was so much harder than I ever thought it would be. I had taken such a practical stance on the moment. After all, we would be together again soon.

If I had known how I would feel from the first time we laid eyes on each other, from our first hug, I would have planned this whole trip differently. I thought I could come, marry Hamoudi, spend some time with him and go back home and bring him as soon as possible. How wrong I was!

As my bus pulled me away from him that hot June day, I couldn't stop my tears from falling. In fact, I cried most of the way home.

The day I left Gaza was one of the hardest days of my life.

From the moment I got back to Canada, all I wanted was for Hamoudi and me to be together again. Children are an amazing gift, and my children helped me to stay focused and they gave me so much of the strength I needed to get through this difficult time.

One evening, I was walking with my daughter, Madeline, who was 14 at the time. We were talking about mom and daughter stuff when she suddenly told me that I was an inspiration to her. I was stunned. How was I an inspiration to her? I had just left her for 3 weeks and had returned home sad and feeling lost. Maddy was quick to explain. "You have wanted to go to Gaza for so long, and now you've finally done it! If you can make your dreams come true, it makes me believe I can do anything too!"

I was speechless. Anything I might have said was caught with the tears in my throat. It was one of my greatest moments as a parent. That night, out on the streets of my hometown, my daughter gave me one of my most precious gifts. She put me back on my feet and made me feel like I was a good mom. I was on top of the world; and more than that, she gave me the motivation I needed to keep going and see this through to the end.

I had been to Gaza, yes, but Hamoudi was still there, and I had not been able to accomplish all that I wanted to.
It was the summer of 2009 by this time. I was home, back at work, and completely heartbroken. I was encouraged that I had been able to accomplish as much as I had, but I knew I wasn't finished yet.

Due to political complications in Gaza between Fatah and Hamas, Hamoudi faced very long delays in getting his passport renewed. It had expired and therefore we were unable to move forward with our immigration application. After getting married, I planned to sponsor him to come and join me in Canada. For years, we had been waiting to be together. Now that we were married, we thought the following steps would be fairly easy.

We were wrong.

The passport delays went on for months and our frustration

grew. Life in Gaza does not give much room for hope, and so Hamoudi came to believe that he would never make it to Canada. I needed him to believe but the suffocating oppression of Gaza took all hope from him. Only I had the strength to believe we would make it through everything. It was hard to hear the sadness and disbelief in Hamoudi's voice, but I was determined to show him that we'd make it through. In the months that followed my return to Canada, it seemed that the only way that we would be together again in the short run would be for me to go back to Gaza. There is no way for the average person in Gaza to come for a visit to Canada. I started working on finding how I would get back there.

The first time I had been to Gaza with Code Pink, Dr. Norm Finkelstein had come up with an idea to have a huge march through Gaza that would join international volunteers with the residents of Gaza. Together, the plan was to create a huge demonstration, made up of thousands of people, to raise the world's awareness of the siege that had kept Gaza closed in since 2006. People were suffering, hospitals were not able to provide necessary health care, and people were dying. Something had to be done.

Over the months that followed, I began speaking in various locations, including churches and my local high school, to raise awareness as well as to raise funds so I could go back to Gaza with the Free Gaza March that was coming at the end of December 2009. I planned to leave home on December 26 so I could spend Christmas with my children and family. I was so sure that this would work out that I just kept moving forward, as if I would be there.

All the money and plans came together in time for me to board a KLM flight out of Vancouver right after Christmas. I stopped over in Amsterdam and carried on to Cairo. There, I met up with my Gaza March colleagues and we prepared to make our way to Gaza.

Once in Cairo, word spread through the group that the government representatives from, ... most of the embassies had communicated with each other to agree that no one would be allowed to cross into Gaza. We were horrified and disappointed. Well, I was horrified. One of our group members from Portugal even told us that his embassy had called him on his cell phone (how did they get his cell phone number???) to tell him not to go to Gaza.

Of course, we were more determined than ever to make it! Most of the group wanted to go to Gaza as a political statement against the siege, but for me, it was a lot more personal. My husband was still in Gaza, and we had not been together in 6 months! For me, the news from the embassies was hard to believe and it left me feeling stunned and cold. Hamoudi and I needed to be together.

I stayed at the Sun Hotel just off Tahrir Square in Cairo. My roommates were some of the most wonderful women I could have spent time with.

There was Joanne, who spent time with Christian Peacemaker Teams in the West Bank and in Iraq; Pat, who taught me that nuns are NOT who I thought they were! She had also spent time working with CPT as well as other peace organizations. I also stayed with Alice, who was boisterous and friendly. She always had something to say in every situation. I am so sorry that I cannot remember the name of my fourth roommate but what I do remember is that all of these women are about the same age as my mother and I felt warm and safe in their company. These women are what I aspire to be as I continue on in my life.

I love them like they are my own family. I had been Pat's

roommate in Cairo on my first trip to Gaza and had gotten to know Joanne and Pat both on that first trip.

I am grateful for the gift that each of these women was to me during that difficult time in Egypt. These women were always full of wisdom and words of encouragement. I felt like I had four much needed moms when my own mom was on the other side of the world.

We faced all of the adventures in Cairo together. When we realized that all the embassies had pulled together against us, we leaned on each other and our friendship grew through those many days we spent together.

We could not get out of Cairo as a group. There was no way the Egyptian authorities were going to let us leave. At one point, a small group decided to try to make it across the border. By this time, I was so confused and felt so lost that I didn't know what to do. There was so much controversy about this small group that I felt like I shouldn't join them. I stayed away from the crowd that day but learned later that they had expected me to be on that bus. Again, I cried. My tears of frustration and disappointment were becoming my common companion. If there's one thing that there is a lot of in Gaza, it's frustration and disappointment. It was another lesson of growth for me.

Finally, it was time for most of the people who had come to Cairo to now go home. They had planned for a certain number of days and now all those days had passed. I could not leave, however. I had to try to get into Gaza.

I thought that getting on the bus and heading for Rafah myself would be my best chance at getting to Gaza. I had my marriage certificate to prove my justification for being allowed to cross the border. I was nervous as I boarded the bus that day but hopeful that my trip would end well.

It takes about 5 hours to travel from Cairo, through the Sinai to Al Arish and the seats are so close together that there is no room to stretch out my legs at all.

Approximately 2 hours into the trip, as we were approaching Ismailia, which is the gateway to the Sinai, the bus had to stop at a security checkpoint manned by armed Egyptian security guards.

Two of them boarded the bus and slowly walked down the aisle, asking to see everyone's ID. When the security guard came to my seat, I showed him my passport. He took it with him when he got off the bus. I was nervous but wanted to look calm. I did not want to draw any unnecessary attention to myself.

The security guards held the bus at their checkpoint for over an hour while I watched my passport change hands as plain clothed security personnel spoke on their cell phones, obviously about me.

Finally, a tall, arrogant young man walked over to me and told me that I was going back to Cairo. I panicked. Hamoudi was 5 hours in one direction and Cairo was 2 hours in the opposite direction.

I showed him my marriage certificate and insisted that I needed to get to Gaza. He didn't make any eye contact and simply said, "No.

There were a large group of uniformed security officers sitting along the curb of the highway and I went to them and spoke, partly in English and partly in Arabic while I waved my marriage certificate, "My husband min Falasteen!!! Ana go

And **Back** Again . . .

Gaza!!! My husband min Falasteen!!!!"

My tears were unstoppable as my panic rose. I was in the middle of nowhere and everywhere there was only armed Egyptian security; and yet I screamed at them, "My husband min Falasteen!!!!"

The younger officers looked miserable and helpless as they watched my meltdown but the plain clothed arrogant officer was unmoved.

I called Hamoudi and was crying so much I could hardly speak.

"What's wrong, baby?" he asked, already knowing the answer. "They won't let me come!!" I blurted out through my tears. Hamoudi and I felt so helpless, so devastated. There was no way around the Egyptian security. If they wouldn't let me past, I was not getting past. Hamoudi and I were 5 hours from each other, but we were worlds apart.

I continued to beg for some understanding from the uniformed security officers but to no avail.

The tall, arrogant officer finally told me that I could come back another day and get to Gaza. I jumped on his words for the tiniest shred of hope.

"When? When can I come back and get to Gaza?"

Without looking at me, he replied, "In 3 days and I promise, you'll get to Gaza"

I took a deep breath and thanked him – until I saw what was to happen next. I learned later that his promise of my entry in 3 days was simply to get me to go away.

For the **Love** of Hamoudi

This security officer walked out onto the Cairo-bound side of the highway and waved down a vehicle, any vehicle. I was stunned.

The driver stopped and the officer told me to get in. I protested. I did not know the driver; I did not want to go to Cairo! The officer became angry with me and insisted that I get in the van. The driver of the van was also becoming impatient with me as I continued to protest.

It became obvious to me that there was no other choice for me but to get in the van that would take me far from my beloved Hamoudi.

Those two hours back to Cairo felt like sandpaper against my skin. I was in pain as I thought of Hamoudi sitting on his side of the border waiting for me.

Once again, God provided for me in this terrible moment. On the same bus that I was on, there was a man from the United States who had also intended to go to Gaza. He, too, was forced to get in the van with me and head back to Cairo. He tried to comfort me as he saw my distress and realized my reason for needing to continue heading north instead of being forced onto that van.

When we got to the outskirts of Cairo, the van driver told us to get out. I had no idea where we were at that point, and then the driver insisted that we each pay him 100 Egyptian pounds. I was incensed! 100 Egyptian pounds to be abducted and forced away from my husband?? I refused to pay.

The driver became angry and insisted that I pay. I reached into my pocket and pulled out a 5 Egyptian pound note and offered it to the driver. He scoffed at it and refused to take it. I told him that if he wanted to get paid, he should go and ask the Egyptian security officer who forced me to ride in his van to pay him. The driver looked at me like I was crazy!

Finally, the American man negotiated payment for both of us that the driver would accept and the van left us on the side of the road. A taxi came along in a few minutes and took us into Cairo and back to our hotel.

It wasn't long before I planned another attempt. I just had to wait for Egyptian security to calm down from having all the foreign activists in Cairo. Once they had calmed down, I was sure I would make it to the border and take my chances with the border police. Until then, I had a few days in Cairo to try to figure out what I should do to ensure success next time.
I visited the Canadian embassy in hopes that they would see my marriage certificate and, at least, let me pay them to write me a letter of waiver which I understood that the border police would sometimes accept and allow a person to cross into Gaza.

The woman at the embassy was kind but condescending. She then offered to help me with Hamoudi's immigration papers. I was so encouraged. I was happy to take whatever help they would give us! She told me to make an appointment for the next day and come back to the embassy.

I came back, excited for the promised help that we so desperately needed! When she and I were alone in the office, ready for our meeting, I pulled out the thick stack of papers that were the immigration application with my marriage certificate.

The woman asked for Hamoudi's phone number and called him for me. When he answered, she handed me the phone and then left the room. Where was our help?
I had told Hamoudi that this phone call would be our help

filling out our application. Government paperwork is so confusing and even more so when one is under so much stress.

We made the most of our phone call, realizing that we weren't getting any help but also very aware that we were not paying for this precious conversation. We talked for close to an hour and had to wrap it up when the embassy representative came back into the room.

I felt better after talking to Hamoudi and my determination to get to Gaza was renewed. I would not be discouraged, no matter what happened.

After a few days, I was hoping that Egyptian security had calmed down after our big group had left town. I was hoping that I could at least make it to the border and have the opportunity to show my paperwork to the border guards. I was sure, in that case, that I would be allowed to cross into Gaza.

The bus made one stop along the route at a small restaurant. The washrooms were horrible! They were nothing more than holes in the very dirty floor. However, when you gotta go, you gotta go! I made the best of it, and quickly finished, trying to forget the unpleasantness of that moment.

As an obvious foreigner, everyone stared at me like I was from Outer Space. Men, especially, looked at me as if I should want them to be looking at me. One man sat at the same table as me and started asking a lot of questions. I had spent enough time in Egypt to be suspicious of anyone who asked me too many personal questions. I kept my answers short and vague.

We got back on the bus and continued our journey north. The

bus seats were so close together that my legs got hopelessly cramped during those long hours on the road.

I tried moving a little to relieve the pain in my legs but there was nowhere to move. The person sitting beside me was so close that almost any movement would have me bumping into him – something that I tried desperately to avoid and was usually successful.

Finally, our bus arrived in Al Arish, an Egyptian town that is about half an hour from the Gaza border. This is where I would get off and spend the night and head for the border the next morning.

I stayed at a small "hotel" called the Mecca Hotel. The rooms cost about the same as I paid in Cairo – just over $10 a night. The Mecca Hotel was much nicer than my accommodations in Cairo, however. In comparison, the rooms were luxurious and the town I was in had that distinctive small town feel. The people were so friendly and helpful in Al Arish. It was a good place to relax and calm down after a stressful trip.

The dining room provided a delicious breakfast, although I only recognized the pita bread and nothing else. It felt good to have a decent breakfast in such a friendly place before embarking on another try at the border. I was nervous, actually scared, but determined not to turn back until I had made it to Gaza. This day started out with such promise, including a good meal and helpful staff at the hotel. I could never have imagined what the next couple of hours would hold for me.

My taxi driver that morning was a very kind man who assured me that he would translate for me once we got to the border at Rafah. When we arrived, the border police tried to turn us around before we even got to the gate. I insisted we move as far forward as we could. The border police were not interested in my reason for being there; they just wanted me to leave. I refused.

They told my driver that the border was closed. I told them that it was urgent that I be allowed to get into Gaza. I showed them my marriage certificate and explained that my husband was in Gaza and that we hadn't seen each other in six months. No one cared. They told me to leave. I grew desperate. I urged my driver to continue translating for me even though he just wanted to get as far from those border police as possible.

Finally, the man I was addressing told me that my marriage certificate wasn't enough. At first, he recommended that I get a letter from my embassy asking them to let me cross the border. I replied that there was no way my embassy would issue such a letter, and that they were fully aware of that. Of course, I was right, so the policeman came up with another solution for me. He told me that because my husband is Palestinian, I could go to the Palestinian embassy in Cairo and get a letter from them giving me permission to cross into Gaza. The problem was that Cairo was about six hours back the way I'd just come the day before! Frustration and denials are the order of the day when it comes to trying to cross this border.

My tears couldn't be held back as I explained to the policeman that I had just come from Cairo the day before and that my husband was waiting on the other side of the border; merely a few hundred metres away. I cried and begged and pleaded, on and on. No matter what I said, he would simply refuse to let me cross. My driver begged me to just leave and do as I was told. This was so common in Egypt; to just do as one was told by the authorities. There was so much fear in this country with regard to those in power. While our group was holding demonstrations in Cairo, our Egyptian friends were afraid to take part, and when they wanted to hold their own demonstration, they asked if as many of us visitors as possible would join them. They ran a high risk of arrest and torture for speaking out.

After a lot of debate with the border police, I saw the pleading in my driver's eyes and decided to back down and get the letter the policeman recommended I get from the Palestinian embassy in Cairo. With much sadness and frustration I went back to that friendly little hotel in Al Arish. The staff was hoping they wouldn't see me again that day, knowing my destination, and they all sympathized with my disappointment when I arrived to stay for another night.

I called Hamoudi as I was leaving the border. He had been waiting for me on the other side. Even though we had not been able to get together that day, it felt like we were being torn apart again. I cried all the way back to Al Arish. This was so unfair! I had our original marriage certificate, which was written in Arabic. That policeman could read every word of it and he KNEW that I was only trying to be reunited with my husband. The frustration I experienced was like nothing I had known before. As a Canadian, the only border I was used to crossing was the Canada/US border, from which I had never been refused! I had even been to this border on my previous trip and had no trouble at all in getting across. I didn't understand; I couldn't accept this. My heart burned with agony as I paid the taxi driver without trying to bargain with him at all. He had gone above and beyond what would ever be expected of him. He had really put himself on the line for me with those policemen. He could have easily been arrested for talking back to them, even though it was on my behalf. Egypt is a harsh country. It looks so romantic when you read about it in travel magazines but I was being confronted by a very different Egypt; a harder, colder Egypt that I had ever heard of before. I had met the taxi drivers who tried to charge me too much, the perfume sellers who tried to charge me too much and the sellers in the market who tried to charge me too much, and chalked it all up to an interesting cultural experience but now that I had a little more experience with knowing the Egyptian police, I realized that there was also a darker, more sinister side to this beautiful country that would be hard to get used to.

My journey back to Cairo was uneventful. I didn't want to talk to anyone and I didn't want anyone to talk to me. My noble motivation for making this trip seemed so irrelevant to me now. Why was I denied at the border? What was I supposed to do now? I cried out to God again and again, begging Him to make sense of all of this agony for me. My heart was full and aching and my mind was spinning as I sat in silent disbelief on that long, lonely road back to Cairo.

I returned to the Sun Hotel and dragged my bags back to my room. The staff smiled and assured me that "next time" I would certainly make it across to Gaza. They seemed to either not understand or not believe that their own policemen would act in such a way at the border. As soon as I landed, I asked for directions to the Palestinian embassy, or "safarat falasteen" as I learned to ask in Arabic.

The next morning, I got up early and went down to the street to get over to the Palestinian embassy. The clerk at my hotel recommended that I take the Metro (underground transit train) to the part of the city where the embassy was and just take a taxi from where I get off the train to save myself what would be a hefty taxi fare.

I paid one Egyptian pound (about 25 cents Canadian) to take the train across Cairo to the right section of the city then another 5 pounds for the taxi to deliver me to the door of the

And **Back** Again . . .

Palestinian Embassy. I was warmly welcomed and invited to come straight into the office of the Palestinian representative, Mr. El Farra, who had recently arrived at work for the day.

When I explained the nature of my visit, he sighed deeply and called for some tea for us. Palestinian hospitality never fails in every situation. We talked at length, Mr. El Farra handing me a tissue when I could no longer hold back my tears. His gentleness and kindness helped me feel somewhat confident as I shared my need to get to Gaza.

Mr. El Farra called the embassy lawyer into his office and told him about my plight. He then called his Egyptian colleagues to confirm that a letter from him would be enough to get me across the border. As he told me, his signature and time are worth too much to spend on a task that would accomplish nothing. After getting off the phone, he assured me that this letter would, indeed, be accepted once I got back to the border with it. I could expect to be in Hamoudi's arms the next day! I was so happy and relieved. The kindness showed me in that office soothed my raw emotions from the previous day.

Mr. El Farra asked his lawyer to draw up a letter on official letterhead that they both signed and stamped with their embassy stamp. I felt like I was holding a goldmine as I left the Palestinian embassy that day!

I walked back to the Metro station, having observed the taxi driver's route carefully on the way there. I jumped on the train, and practically floated all the way back to my hotel! I was going to see Hamoudi in two days! After all I had been through, two more days was not too much to ask! I was so excited as I climbed into bed that night, "Two more days! Back on the bus tomorrow and into Gaza the day after!!" My wait would finally be over.

That afternoon, I had gone to the bus station and bought my ticket to Al Arish for the next morning. I had excitedly shared my news with the hotel clerks and they were very happy for me. All of us together believed that I had finally gathered all that I needed to ... be reunited with Hamoudi.

The next morning, I woke up in the darkness to make sure I wouldn't be late for my bus. I was nervous but excited as I clutched that precious letter in my shaking hands. This was it. This would be my last trip and I would cross that difficult border and continue my mission side by side with my beloved husband.

I boarded the bus ... and set off across the Sinai ... to try again to cross the border. This time, though, I had legal, written permission in my hand. This time, I would get through for sure and this time, I would not face the same agony and frustration that I had met before.

Through all of the hours that I traveled through Egypt, past all the now familiar landmarks, I clutched Mr. El Farra's letter to my heart. I pictured the joy that Hamoudi and I would share when I finally walked through the gate of the Palestinian border terminal. The next day would be very, very good. I just had to get to Al Arish and spend one more night alone. It was only a number of hours until I'd be back in my husband's arms.

When I walked into the Mecca Hotel in Al Arish, Egypt, I was greeted warmly, as an old friend. I felt calm and relaxed. I explained to my friends there that I had gotten a letter, as instructed by the Egyptian border police, from the Palestinian embassy in Cairo. They were impressed that I had gotten the letter so quickly and was already back in Al Arish to try again to get into Gaza. They were not accustomed to seeing a woman with such tenacity, such determination. Neither were they accustomed to seeing a woman who loved her husband enough to go through as much as I had. They often told me that they would have thought that I would just quit and go home. This life was too hard, too frustrating, and too painful to be worth it for anyone. Perhaps it was because I was western that they were amazed. The impression of westerners, I've learned, was that we were godless and promiscuous and certainly not devoted to our spouses like they were seeing in this woman in front of them. I was a mystery.

In one conversation in Cairo with an Egyptian friend of a colleague of mine, after I explained the values and principles of Christians, he said in stunned amazement, "Well, you're just like us". He had thought that they and not we were the ones with morals and values for our behaviour and lives. His whole understanding of western Christians was shaken up that day.

All of that was behind me now as I prepared for my entry back into Gaza.
I woke up that day full of excitement and emotion. I had not seen Hamoudi in six months when we were so painfully pulled apart at the Gaza side of this Rafah border. Now was the day for our reunion!

I happily ate breakfast and cheerfully said my goodbyes to the staff at the Mecca Hotel. I had shown them my letter and they too were sure that this would be enough to get me through. They had seen me through my failed attempts to get back but today, everyone was confident with me that this was the last time we'd see each other for a long time.

The front desk clerk called a taxi for me and I waited with eager anticipation. Finally he arrived and loaded in my bags and I was on my way! As we drove that last 20 minutes or

For the **Love** of Hamoudi

so to the border, my heart was dancing as we closed the distance between Hamoudi and me.

Once at the border, I smiled as I climbed out of the cab, making sure my letter was in my hand and not tucked away in any of my bags.

I walked up to the gate and smiled as I showed the letter to the Egyptian border police. I was about to be in Gaza again! This was too surreal, a dream of a lifetime coming true AGAIN! I stood in the north Sinai sun waiting as the officer read my letter. I thought about my visit at the Palestinian embassy, my long tiring bus trips back and forth through Egypt and I thought of Hamoudi, waiting on the other side of this border. As exhausted as I was, it was all worth it as I stood at this moment, ready to move forward with Hamoudi.

"This means nothing to us. You need a letter from your own embassy." His words were like a knife in my heart. I suddenly felt weak and helpless. I had traveled so many hours, back and forth, to do exactly as I was told and now they were telling me that they won't accept this letter? The Palestinian ambassador had even called his Egyptian counterparts to make sure that this letter would be accepted at the border but I was so far from Cairo now and the border police make their own rules about who gets across this border and who gets turned back.

I couldn't believe what I was hearing. "No no, I was told TWO DAYS AGO to go to the Palestinian embassy, safarat falasteen, to get THIS letter and I've done that. I was HERE two days ago and I went all the way back to Cairo and went to the Palestinian embassy and now have come all the way back here. This is the letter that YOU PEOPLE asked for and I have it!!" I was even too shocked to cry at that moment. The border officer again told me that because I'm Canadian,

112

I need a letter from the Canadian embassy, which, of course, I would never be able to get. I told him that because I am married to a Palestinian, and I showed him my marriage certificate, that the letter from the Palestinian embassy was valid. He didn't care. I started to cry.

I had the correct documentation in my hand, I had jumped through the hoops as instructed, and yet, here I stood; denied again. This was, indeed, a harsh and unpredictable land. I couldn't bring myself to turn around and leave the border. I had done everything I was told to do in order to be able to cross. I was frozen in stunned disbelief. Fortunately, I was too shocked to immediately notice that agony welling up in my chest and filling up even my arms and legs.

The longer I tried to reason with the police officer, the more the reality of my situation sunk in. I started to shake; I felt my tears rising up inside me on the crest of a scream, which I had to push back down.

Where was God in this moment? Why was He allowing this to happen? What about all the miles I'd traveled? What about all the hours I'd spent cramped in those seats on the buses? Didn't God care about any of that? Why didn't He open the gates and let me in?

I was speechless through my tears and finally walked away. Eventually I came to understand and accept that I was not getting into Gaza that day. I could barely stand up but forced my legs to carry me away from the border gates and back to where I could find a taxi to take me back to Al Arish and on to Cairo. Again.

For the **Love** of Hamoudi

Chapter Eight

There's More Than One Way to Cross the Sinai

Once back in Cairo, I knew I had to come up with another plan. I had always believed the saying, "insanity is doing the same thing over and over again and expecting a different result". It made no sense to try again in the same way. I needed to take a few days to catch my breath and find another way to get to the border. I simply could not risk the many check points along the main highway again. Getting pulled off the bus for unknown reasons, for an unknown length of time was too stressful and scary, since I was traveling alone.

I spoke to some of my friends who were also in Cairo, trying to see if any of their contacts would be able to get them into Gaza. So far, no one was successful.

One of my colleagues was willing to come with me on my next attempt since she, also, had not been able to get another way into Gaza.

I asked Mahmoud, the front desk clerk at the Sun Hotel in Tahrir Square in Cairo, if he knew anything about taking the bus to Al Arish via Taba instead of straight from Cairo. Taba is a long way southeast of Cairo and there is a border crossing there to take travelers to Israel. It would mean another bus ride but possible success, so it would be worth the try. I couldn't leave Egypt without knowing that I had tried everything I could. Until then, there would be another bus ride.

I went to the bus station immediately to buy our tickets for Taba in preparation for leaving the next evening. The Taba bus trip was an overnighter, leaving Cairo at about 10pm and arriving in Taba at about 5am. Mahmoud assured us that once we arrived in Taba, there would be another bus to take us to Al Arish. Everything would be alright.

None of it mattered to me. I kept thinking that, as hard as all of this was on me, it must be so much harder on Hamoudi, sitting in Gaza unable to leave and unable to help me enter. I would do whatever I could think of to try to get us together as long as I was in Egypt. God hadn't made this path easy, but He made me tenacious enough to face each difficult step.

Pam and I got to the Turkoman bus station in Cairo early enough to make sure we made it on our bus. I was, once again, full of hope. She had a laptop computer with her that she wanted to give to a friend of hers in Gaza. We pulled all of our bags out of the taxi, paid the driver and dragged all of our belongings into the bus station. After we sat down in the waiting area for Taba passengers, Pam looked around and noticed that the laptop she was carrying wasn't with her. She soon realized that she had not taken it out of the trunk of the taxi. We had waiting on the curb while the driver removed our things and didn't think to double check to make sure we had everything.

I didn't know what to say. Pam said that she didn't even want to go to Gaza anymore if she didn't have that computer with her. I was speechless. I was desperate to get there and I couldn't be held up because of a misplaced computer. I tried to be cheerful and positive but it wasn't working. It was going to be a very long trip to Taba that night.

We finally arrived at around 5am, before the January sun was even thinking of waking up. It was very hard to see, but not so hard that I couldn't make out the fact that there was nothing there! The small building that was used as a bus station was in total darkness. No one was working there. We asked around for when the next bus was coming but we couldn't find anyone who spoke enough English to help us with our predicament.

Finally, one of the drivers who came in to pick up the people who were dropped off there, took the time to try to help us. He and I used mostly sign language between us, I also used some English, he, some Arabic, but we somehow understood each other.

There was no bus to Al Arish. Period.

Our only chance of getting to Al Arish was to take a taxi but from Taba, which was another 6 or 7 hours. It would cost us about 600 Egyptian pounds each. We didn't have that much on us.

That driver and I argued and negotiated for some time and finally he accepted 300 pounds each from us. I told him we had no money with us and we were stuck and had to get to Al Arish. He asked me cautiously if we were actually going to Rafah. I hesitated but quickly realized that I had no choice but to trust this man so I slowly nodded my head.

He looked serious for a moment but then picked up our bags and loaded them into the back of his van. We were on our way to Al Arish with a rough looking little man who seemed to know his way very well around that part of the Sinai.

For the **Love** of Hamoudi

The scenery was breathtaking as we traveled mile after mile through the desert. The terrain was rough in some parts, much like the people who live here. I saw herders and their flocks walking across the sand, somehow finding food. I also saw foxes running from place to place. I thought of that verse in the Bible, "the foxes have holes but the Son of Man has no place to lay His head." These would have been the same kind of foxes that were referred to in the Bible. It was truly awe-inspiring to speed through that rugged place. How did anyone survive out here? Yet, we saw many people, here and there, as we made our way along that road.

We approached our first check point. The Egyptian military has check points all through the country, and this road was no exception. Our driver was obviously familiar with the men who stopped him and told them whatever they needed to hear about the nature of our journey. I found it unnerving how the security officers carefully looked through the windows of the van, inspecting everything to see what this driver was carrying. The officers always asked about Pam and me and, although she is American, our driver usually said "Canada" first and we were waived through.

Check point after check point, our driver did all the talking for us. I don't know what he said, exactly, but whatever it was; it was enough to avert any suspicion as to our destination.

I soon came to believe that our driver was actually a smuggler, and from his dress and looks, we guessed he was probably a Bedouin. I prayed that we would arrive in Al Arish safely. I imagined the stories I would later tell about this ride through the desert in the care of a Bedouin smuggler. Who better to get us past the check points and the hours of harsh terrain but someone like him? I thanked God for sending this unusual angel at a time when I needed an angel very badly. Angels come in all shapes, sizes and colours. The fact that my angel happened to be in the form of a smuggler didn't make him any less of an angel. God was, once again, interceding for my safety.

The closer we got to Al Arish, the more difficult it was for the driver to talk his way through the security officers. Finally, he had to give them the name of our hotel in Al Arish. The problem was, we didn't have a hotel booked in Al Arish. Our plan had been to go straight to Rafah.

In our complicated way of communicating, the driver explained to me that the Egyptian security officers were suspicious so we would have to spend some time in Al Arish so they would believe we were staying there. It would be too dangerous for us to go straight to the border that day.

I have no idea how I understood all of that but I was grateful for his experience with these matters. He never once let on to the security officers that our final destination was Gaza. This would have surely gotten us detained and sent back to Cairo.

When I explained all of this to Pam, we agreed that this driver was well worth the full amount he had originally asked for so we planned to stop by a bank, once we arrived in Al Arish, so we could take out more money to pay him. I told him that we needed to find a bank before we went to the hotel. He smiled and nodded. I felt a lot better about our whole arrangement knowing that we would be paying him more than we had finally agreed on.

When we arrived in Al Arish, he took us straight to the Mecca Hotel! I was so happy to be in the company of familiar faces again! The driver spoke to the desk clerk briefly, then he smiled and waved at and started to leave. I told him that we need to go to a bank for more money. He smiled and told me that the hotel can call a taxi for us to do whatever we needed to do, and then he left.

I stood and watched him go. This man had been so gracious. He had literally saved us in the middle of nowhere and now he was gone. To this day, I am convinced that he really was an angel who was sent to ensure our safe passage from Taba to Al Arish that day.

We slept comfortably that night and prepared to hit the border again the next morning. I was losing track of how many times I had tried this and I was losing my sense of excitement over the experience. I ate as much breakfast as I could and gathered my bags together. Maybe today would be the day I finally got to Gaza and saw my husband again. Pam and I stepped out of the cab and approached the border officers. I had my marriage certificate and my letter from the Palestinian embassy in Cairo. I was going to try again.

We told them that we needed to get into Gaza. Pam had gone to the American embassy and had gotten a waiver letter from them, which we had been told was also required by the border police.

We were well armed with paperwork, and started showing it as we started talking.

As soon as we said we want to go to Gaza, the officer shook his head. No. This was all getting to be too much for me. "What do you mean, No?? I have all my paperwork in order. Pam has her letter. We are just two people and we need to get to Gaza" The officer shook his head. I walked away from him because I wanted to cry and scream. This was unreal.

There is a small café (of sorts) at the Rafah border. It is run by a rough looking man and a couple of women who claim to be his wives. There are many children and teenagers running around who seem to belong with the adults, but it's hard to say. This man seems to be in charge of the mob of teenage boys who swarm all the cars that arrive at the border and take off all the luggage and then demand to be paid for it before they will give it back. I held tightly onto my bags when we arrived.

A man came over to me and seemed like he was trying to help. He was frustrated that I didn't speak Arabic so I called Hamoudi so they could talk. If this man would help me get to Gaza, I wanted to know what he had to say.

I called Hamoudi and explained what was going on. He was upset and frustrated but listened as I told him about this man with the café. I told him that I wanted him to talk to this man since I had no idea what this man was saying to me. I passed the man the phone and he and Hamoudi started talking. Finally the man handed the phone back to me. Hamoudi was breathless. "Get away from that man! He is trying to rip us off by charging us to get you to Gaza through the tunnels. Don't talk to him anymore and DON'T GO WITH HIM!!"

I quickly moved away from the café, taking my bags with me. This man and the boys kept trying to take my bags but I hung on for dear life and told Pam to do the same. Hamoudi had also told me that it was no use to talk to the border police about this man since they were all in business together.

I tried again to talk to the border police about getting into the border terminal and seeing about getting to Gaza. The police who are outside are not the border officials who stay inside the terminal. However, if the police refuse to let you past the outside gate, then you have no chance of taking up your case with the border officials, who actually have the power to let a person through. The border police do have the power to decide who they will allow into the terminal and on that day, they had, again, decided that it would not be Pam and me. It was back to Cairo the next day.

I could not understand God's reasoning behind all of this frustration and denials. What was going on? I believe in the God who parted the Red Sea. I believe in the God who created everything and put me here. I believe in the God who knows me personally and cares about me. But here I was traveling back and forth across Egypt, covering more miles than I cared to count, for nothing. Nothing? It was impossible! There had to be some better end to all of this than what I was seeing.

When I got back to Cairo, I took some time to reorganize my thoughts and my plans. I had been in touch with Rev. Alex Awad from Bethlehem, and with Rev. Hanna Massad in Jordan. They, as well as the church leadership in Gaza were praying for me as I continued knocking on this very stubborn door.

My friends in Bethlehem told me that if I could get there, they would try to get me into Gaza through their means. I just needed to get to Bethlehem first. It would mean going a long way out of my way but it would be worth it for so many reasons. The first reason is that I would finally end up in Gaza and, of course, other reasons were that I'd be able to be in Bethlehem and meet some amazing people in person. My next plan was to go to Taba again, but this time, going across the border to Israel and making my way to Bethlehem from there. I was nervous but confident that this was a good thing to do. I had filled out the necessary forms and sent them back to my friends in Bethlehem and was ready to go. There had been heavy rains in the Sinai and the road to Taba was flooded so all of the buses were temporarily grounded. I had to wait a few days for the roads to clear up, but then was able to buy my ticket for Taba; again. I was not going to be discouraged. I was going to finish this … one way or another. Before I boarded the bus for Taba that evening, I double checked that the roads were clear and we'd be able to get through. I was assured that this was the case. My heart was racing as I climbed on the bus. I would cross into Israel this time and then go to Bethlehem!! Tears filled my eyes at the thought of the amazing journey that lay ahead. Reverends Awad and Massad felt like brothers or uncles to me and I couldn't wait to meet them! Of course, it would be more challenging to meet Rev. Massad, since Israel did not allow him to visit in the West Bank at all. I would be able to meet Rev. Awad and visit Bethlehem Bible College! I booked a room there for a night so I could relax and meet as many people as possible. I wanted to hear their stories too!

The words of encouragement I'd been receiving from these men had really been instrumental in keeping me afloat through the many hardships and frustrations I'd been facing along the way. I couldn't wait to thank them for their kind support.

As the bus pulled out of Cairo that night, my thoughts raced as I contemplated the long road ahead. It would be most interesting to have the opportunity to see the West Bank and Gaza in the same trip. This is virtually impossible, but that was the plan; and I had help waiting for me this time.

Sometime in the middle of the night, our bus came to a halt. It was too dark out to see where we were so I had no idea why we had stopped. I listened to some of the other passengers, but everyone only spoke Arabic, so nothing I heard made our situation any more clear to me. I finally, learned that the road was closed due to the flooding in this part of the Sinai. We had to sit here until it was light enough for the driver to see the road. Out here in the middle of the desert, night was very dark and, being that it was January, daylight arrived later in the morning than I would have liked.

We sat there for hours and soon were surrounded by many other vehicles that also had to wait for day light to navigate the treacherous roads. The flooding had spread sand all over the roads and, in some parts, it was very hard to even see where the road was. In the dark, this would have been impossible.

We finally got on our way when the day was light enough to see clearly. I was relieved to be getting closer to Taba and, eventually, Bethlehem. Our ill-maintained bus rattled and chugged along that desert highway. We were now hours behind schedule and I just hoped that we would get to Taba in time for me to catch the border open. I didn't know if they had specific hours they stayed open like the border at Rafah did. Suddenly, the bus surged and let out a loud bang. The people at the back quickly turned around and looked out the back window and were talking excitedly to each other. The driver pulled over to the side of the road and everyone began to gather their belongings together and climb down off of the bus. I didn't know what was happening. It took me a few minutes to figure out that the bus was dead but it took me a lot longer to figure out what we were supposed to do next. Once outside the bus, I collected my luggage and tried to find out what was happening. There was a long streak of some kind of fluid behind the bus so I could only imagine that something had blown out which left us on the side of this highway in the middle of nowhere.

Finally, another bus came into view and a murmur rippled through the crowd of stranded passengers. I could understand the word, "Neweiba", which was one of the destinations of the buses that go along this way. The buses went to Neweiba and Taba, so I knew that this was not my bus. I held onto my luggage and stood back while other people rushed to board this bus when it stopped to take on extra travelers.

As we stood in the sun on the side of the road, I was panicking at the thought of not getting on a bus heading to Taba. I listened very hard to the group of people every time a bus would pull up. I would ask the people around me, "Taba? Taba?", as I pointed to the coming bus. Finally, I was given the nod to get on the next bus!

As we approached the door, it was obvious that the bus was already filled. Every seat already had a body in it. This was no problem for the driver. He continued to wave people onboard and everyone just went as far back down the aisle as they could and held on to whatever they could put their hands on. By the time I got on, the aisle and stairs were already filled so I had to turn and sit on the dashboard of the bus. Two more people got on after me and they stood in the stairway leading to the door, which didn't close quite properly. I was certainly not in Canada anymore!

The driver slowly pulled his old bus back onto the highway and we continued our journey towards Taba. As I hung on to my position for dear life, I started to laugh at the situation. Here I was, sitting on the dashboard of a rundown Egyptian travel bus after getting stranded by a broken down bus in the middle of nowhere! As I sat there, my body moving to the rhythm of the road, I realized what I resembled!

I look at the Australian man who was facing me from the stairs and said, smiling, "I'm the bobble head!" He paused for a moment, looking at me, trying to figure out what I was referring to. He said, "What?" "I'm the bobble head! You know" and I mimicked the many bobble heads I'd seen on many, many dashboards at home. I posed at the front of the bus and let my head bounce loosely as we drove over the bumpy road. The Australian began to laugh, "Yes you are!"

For the **Love** of Hamoudi

When we got to the check point that was close to Taba, our driver was about to be reprimanded by the security officers there. I don't speak Arabic, but I do understand tone of voice and body language. The driver explained our predicament and the officers left him alone.

We showed our passports or ID cards, whichever we had, and continued on our way.

We finally arrived in Taba around noon that day. It had taken fourteen hours to make this seven hour trip, and I was exhausted. My day, however, was far from over. It was a short trip to the Israeli border and I wanted to get through that day since there was really nothing much around the bus terminal except a place to get some lunch. I grabbed my luggage and found a taxi that was taking people to the border.

The border terminal there was very modern, like something we'd expect to find around home. I walked up to the first officer and told her I was heading for Bethlehem. She asked for my passport. In my passport, are stamps to show that I had entered Gaza through Rafah the previous summer. She asked me why I had gone to Gaza. Of course, I didn't dare tell her about Hamoudi but I did tell her about the church there that I visited. "There are Christians in Gaza?" she said, as if mocking me. "No, I don't think so".

I was surprised by her response. I assured her there most definitely were Christians in Gaza, and I had visited them. She called over someone else, who also looked at my passport and the two of them confirmed to each other that what I was saying was impossible. No one would go to Gaza to visit Christians. They simply don't exist. I thought of the people I had gotten to know there and my heart ached for them. They were considered invisible by these Israeli border guards.

There is More than One Way to **Cross** the Sinai

I was sent into an office to talk to a more senior security officer. She, again, asked me about the nature of my trip. I told her I was going to Bethlehem to meet some pastors that I had been in touch with. She asked if I had any children. I told her I have five. She then said that she didn't believe me. A woman "like me" didn't go to visit pastors in Bethlehem. I was curious just what kind of a woman I was and what kind of a woman would go to visit pastors. I told her that as a Christian, it's what God calls me to do, to visit my brothers and sisters in trouble spots. She smiled and, again, wanted to know what was in Gaza. I told her about the church in Gaza and she, too, didn't believe me.

She asked for me to write down my name and email address for her. I am not sure why she needed that, but I have been told that they look up people on Facebook to see what kinds of interests and affiliations they have. My friendships with Palestinians are evident there and my relationship with Hamoudi is also obvious there. When she left the office with my personal information, I pulled out my laptop and got online and shut down my Facebook account. I don't know if I did it in time or not, but I wasn't comfortable with them having access to so much personal information as they would find there. I am not an extremist; I do not condone violent acts of any kind. I am a Christian, and I believe in peace and justice, and I don't mind anyone knowing that. The problem is that these people were not trying to be my friends. They were trying to access as much personal information as possible about me to use against me. To this day I have no idea who got to my Facebook page first.

That same woman came back and questioned me again several times. I had to stay in the border terminal the whole time. I called Rev. Alex Awad to let him know where I was and he told me where I could stay for the night in Israel, close to Taba. I was grateful for his assistance and promised to call again as soon as I was settled in for the night.

Around five in the evening, I approached the security officer who had been questioning me and told her that since I was a woman traveling alone, could they please let me know, one way or another, what their decision would be so I could either proceed into Israel or go back into Egypt while it was still day light. I did not want to be stuck in the middle of the night with no one around who could help me.

She simply told me that it was out of her hands. I didn't believe her, since she seemed to wield a fair amount of authority around there, and everything about me that had been submitted to higher authorities had come through her. I had already been there for four hours by the time I made my first request about getting out.

She kept coming back to ask me the same questions again over the next four hours and finally, at nine o'clock in the evening, she told me that I was an "idealist" and therefore a threat to Israeli security. I would not be allowed in. I was shocked by her logic. An idealist? Isn't that a good thing? Apparently, to Israel, an idealist is a threat, and she took me and escorted me to the exit door. I was thrust outside into the Egyptian night nowhere near any towns or anything. I was immediately set upon by taxi drivers but I was not in the mood to negotiate and I had no idea where I should go. I grabbed my bag, walked past all the waiting taxis and started down the dark road that took me away from the border and into Egypt.

I cried my heart out as I continued down that road. I was alone, scared and had no one to call to come and help me. I called out to God and asked Him to please help me! I kept walking, trying to clear my head and think straight about my present situation. I couldn't think of anything that would help.

There is More than One Way to **Cross** the Sinai

Finally, a taxi driver asked if I wanted to be taken to the nearest town. I had no idea what that was but I couldn't just keep walking in the night. I was alone and it wouldn't be safe for me to just stay on the road. I climbed in the van and told him I couldn't afford to go all the way back to Cairo by taxi so I wanted to find some place close by that would be inexpensive. I would catch the bus back to Cairo in the morning.

He was on his phone to other taxi drivers, trying to find out where would be the best place to take me when we pulled up beside another taxi. He told me that the other driver had passengers who also wanted to stay somewhere locally but would be going to Cairo in the morning. Perhaps I would prefer to ride with them. I knew it would mean a double fare for me, but I didn't care at that moment. I was lonely, sad and exhausted and I could hardly care what happened, just as long as I had some place to sleep.

I climbed into the waiting van, and much to my joy and surprise, the passengers on board were a Canadian gay couple from Montreal! Here I was, alone in the southern Sinai and now I was in the company of a Canadian gay couple! I laughed through my tears at God's wonderful care for me. I was safe. No one would be hitting on me, and these two could speak English, sort of. It turned out that they spoke better French than English but we did ok. I was so relieved to be traveling with them at that point. As I sat in the darkness, traveling down that road, I prayed and asked God to show me what I should do next. I had tried everything, and now I was even kicked out of Israel. In a miraculous moment, I felt His arms around my shoulders and I heard Him say, "NOW you know what it feels like to be Palestinian. You have been rejected for no reason, denied for no reason and turned away from every effort to get to Gaza. This is an experience for you but everyday life for Palestinians."

For the **Love** of Hamoudi

In that moment, I realized that I had learned more than I would have if I had been given the opportunity to sit down in Bethlehem or Gaza to talk about the Palestinian experience. Here I was, sad, frustrated and alone; and I finally understood how my brothers and sisters felt. They, too, were rejected by a large portion of the world, and certainly, a large portion of western Christians. I felt peace in the middle of my heartbreak. I knew it was time to return to Canada. I was not going to get into Gaza this time but I would take home something very valuable; a broken heart.

We went to a rustic resort in Neweiba called Ras Sinai which was like a piece of heaven on earth! I sat on the porch of my cabin and looked out across the Red Sea. I could see the lights of Jordan, Israel and Palestine from there. It all looked so beautiful from a distance. The trouble they were all facing made me feel so much sadder suddenly when I saw so much beauty from a distance.

I breathed in the sea air and slept like a baby. My cabin had tied grass walls and a concrete floor and it only cost me about five dollars for the night. I needed this kind of a place after the day I'd had. It felt like God put His hands on me and soothed away my anxiety and stress with the gentle breezes and fresh aromas. I wish I could have stayed there for a month. I was sure that I could live forever if I could stay in a place like this.

Breakfast the next morning was stunning; a plate full of fresh fruit and cheeses that I didn't recognize – everything was so delicious. We got our bags and walked out to the main road to wait for the bus that would carry us all back to Cairo.
My companions were amazed by my story. We talked all the way back to Cairo. I was so happy to have Canadian friends. I had been in this harsh land for about a month now and I welcomed the little piece of home that these two

represented.

Once back in Cairo, I emailed Rev. Awad to tell him what had happened. There was nothing that any of us could do but his words of encouragement buoyed my spirits as I prepared to return home.

Of course my children were thrilled to have me home but my heart was aching for my husband who was, once again, on the other side of the world. We had gotten within a few hundred metres of each other, but now we were a million miles apart again. I needed a new plan.

I went back to work and kept corresponding with Hamoudi, just as I'd been doing for over eight years by that time.

For the **Love** of Hamoudi

Chapter Nine

One More Try

In the spring of 2009, humanitarian aid ships began to make their way to Gaza. I watched them with great interest but never felt like I should be on them. None of them successfully made port in Gaza and in May, the Turkish aid ship, the Mavi Marmara, was forcefully boarded by the Israeli navy and nine people on board were murdered. This incident caused such an international uproar that there was news that Egypt was being pressured to open its border with Gaza. That's what I needed!

I called the Egyptian embassy in Canada and asked about the border situation at Rafah. The embassy representative told me that the border was open for humanitarian aid organizations and for critically ill patients who needed to get assistance in Egypt. I didn't say anything at the time other than "thank you", but I realized that this situation was no different than it had been before. I was not going to be able to get through this border.

The time came for me to take my vacation from work. I had decided to take two weeks off to work on writing my book. Obviously, I had never written a book to think that I could get it done it two weeks! I discovered something amazing during those two weeks. By taking time off work to create something personal, I began to think and dream. I began to believe again that anything was possible. So, I picked up the phone again to speak to my contact at the Egyptian embassy in Canada. I told him that I wanted to bring a humanitarian group into Gaza, and I needed to know what information he would need from me in order for us to be given permission to enter Gaza. He gave me the list of details and I thanked him very much and hung up.

"What am I thinking?" I laughed at myself as I sat at my kitchen table in my one bedroom basement suite. I was a working mother of five children. I am not famous, I am not wealthy, and I am not powerful. I am not anyone who would be expected to be able to take a group into a place that is impossible to get to.

I sent out a few emails to people that I knew were interested in going to Gaza, and I got enough responses to move forward with submitting our personal information to the Egyptian embassy. I was told it would take about three weeks before we would learn if we had been given permission to enter Gaza through Rafah. There was so much to do!

In those three weeks, my group shrank from ten people down to four. I was worried that we would lose credibility and therefore be refused. Each person who had to withdraw had a valid reason for needing to change their mind, so I called the Egyptian embassy and simply explained the whole story to my contact there. I spoke as if it was all to be expected and he accepted everything I said. He was a bit surprised at the dramatic change in our group size, but didn't say anything to lead me to believe that our group of four had become too small for consideration.

I had also contacted UNRWA in Gaza and asked them for an invitation letter that I could submit to Egypt. Hamoudi knew one of the women who worked there, and when she learned that I was his wife, she happily drafted a letter and got it signed by John Ging, the head of UNRWA in Gaza.

One **More** Try

That letter carried a lot of weight, and in three weeks, I got a call from my contact at the Egyptian embassy. It was seven in the morning and I was in my bathroom brushing my teeth, getting ready for work. My phone rang, and when I saw that the number was from the embassy, I was almost too scared to answer. I quickly cleared out my mouth and answered the phone. The man on the other end told me happily that he had just heard from Cairo and he wanted to let me know that my group had been approved to enter Gaza. My heart was racing and I wanted to scream and shout! I tried to sound professional as I thanked him and hung up. Then I jumped around, laughing. I had to call Hamoudi!

When he answered his phone, I still had not caught my breath and he thought something was wrong. "Are you ok, baby?", he asked with deep concern in his voice. All I could blurt out was "WE'RE APPROVED!" Of course, he knew what I was referring to, and we both laughed and cried and shared our moment of celebration.

It was almost the end of June and I had told the Egyptian government that we'd need to get into Gaza on August 10th. The problem was that without approval, I couldn't get anywhere with fundraising or planning because there was no reason to expect that we would be approved. We were taking a shot in the dark at this but with the pressure on Egypt to soften the border, we were in the right place at the right time; and we were approved!

I told my group to get ready to go. Then I looked at my own situation. I still could not afford another trip to Gaza and yet this was the time to go! Our approval was, indeed, a miracle and I knew that God would give me everything I would need to get there.

On July 1st, I decided to take a day out and I went to our

Canada Day celebration here. There are several at various locations but there is one that has become my favourite over the years. Even though my children wanted to go to the celebration that was closer to home, I wanted to go to the one that was my favourite, so we went our separate ways that day.

While I was walking around looking at all the displays, I came upon a booth that was promoting my union from work. I stopped and talked to the people there and told them what I was doing. I noticed they had a poster up for the Public Service Alliance of Canada's Social Justice Fund. Social Justice Fund? I got excited and asked for more information about this. I told them that this was right in line with what I was doing. The people who were attending the table gave me the email address of the woman who is the local representative for this fund. I was so excited! I couldn't wait to get home and email her to see what she would say.

Through a few exchanges, including a lunch together, the PSAC Social Justice Fund came up with a two thousand dollar donation which covered the cost of my plane ticket. My contribution back to the union would be to speak about my experience at union functions when asked. Nothing could have suited me better!

I bought my ticket and counted the days for my departure. I had been talking to my children about this for months, waiting for the opportunity to open up for me to go. They were all onside with me and were ready to take care of each other while I was away. My children ranged in age from eleven to twenty, and I was confident that they would be able to keep each other going through the next few months.

They were excited for me and assured me that they would be alright while I was in Gaza. I was so torn as I prepared to leave. Leaving my children behind was the hardest part of leaving. As a single parent, I spent my life with my kids. Now I was going away where I couldn't take any of them. I knew this was where I needed to go; that this was what I needed to do or I could have never done it.

We arranged that we would chat online using our cameras so we could see each other as often as we needed to. Hamoudi and I had been doing this for nine years by that time, so I knew it was an effective "second best" way to keep in touch. I wanted to arrive in Cairo a week before we planned to cross the border into Gaza to make sure I had time to translate our paperwork and visit the local government offices to make sure there were no snags in our plan.

I took my UNRWA letter to a local translating service that I had become familiar with on a previous trip to Cairo. Once I had that done, I went to the Ministry of the Interior to see if I could get a letter from them to show to the border police once our group would arrive at Rafah. I had had enough trouble with them to want to take any precautions that I could.

After visiting one government office, I was told that I actually needed to visit a different office. I walked back and forth through Cairo in the August sun trying to minimize our problems at the border. Finally, I got to an office that could give me an answer about the letter I was looking for from them. There would be no such letter.

I was told that if I had been given permission to enter Gaza, then it would be recorded at the border and all I needed to do was to tell the border security and they would look it up and see that I was allowed to enter. I had to be careful how I worded my concerns about trusting the border police but nothing I said was going to get me the letter that would have given me so much peace of mind.

For the **Love** of Hamoudi

I met up with my group, Kit, Ridgley, and Keith, and bought us all bus tickets to Al Arish. I called my friends at the Mecca Hotel there and told them we'd need a room for the night. When the time came, I took a deep breath, hoped for the best, and got on the bus. We were heading for Gaza, we hoped.

Our bus ride was completely uneventful and finally we arrived in Al Arish that afternoon. We checked into our hotel and looked around town a bit, trying hard not to be nervous about the next day.

The following morning, we enjoyed a relaxing breakfast before taking our taxi to the border. Because of the softening of the border, there were a lot of Palestinians trying to get home. Ramadan was going to begin in a couple of days, so we were sure that most of the people wanted to be home with family and friends before that.

We finally got through the crowd to talk to the border police. Our friend, Aiman, from Al Arish, came with us to translate. From my previous experience, I believed that having a translator would help us a lot. The officers had been very rude to me when they learned that I didn't speak Arabic. We needed all the advantages we would think of. I had already gotten our paperwork translated into Arabic, but was concerned that wouldn't help us if we weren't able to speak to the officers at the gate.

As expected, we were first told to go to our embassies and get letters from them. The officer didn't listen to anything we said about having permission to enter. I told him that we didn't need to go to our embassies because Cairo had already given us permission. He told us again to get letters. Aiman was a little nervous because, in Egypt, you do as you're told and don't argue with the police. I urged him to tell the officer that we had permission and that he needed to check with the officials in the terminal to confirm that. Aiman hesitantly told the officer what I had said. The officer finally agreed to take our passports and call to see if we have permission. He told us to stand to the side and wait until he called us.

As we stood back and allowed the Palestinians who were coming back to Gaza to continue on their way, I was appalled by what I saw.

The Egyptian border police screamed at an elderly woman, and almost stepped on a child who I quickly pulled out of the way. One young woman arrived by taxi, obviously having just been released from a hospital from having leg surgery. Her foot was in an apparatus that was screwed into her shin bone. That, in itself, was hard enough to watch, but then this young woman had to get out of her taxi and walk to the front gate and then continue the few hundred metres to the terminal. From there, she would have to walk through the building, climb onto a bus and then walk through the Palestinian border terminal. Hopefully, by the time she got that far, someone would have a wheelchair for her.

I started to cry as I watched the continued abuse of the Palestinians who were returning home or going to visit family. I caught my breath and dried my tears though. I thought to myself that this pain was theirs and not mine. I had no right to shed tears if they were strong enough to get through this. I looked around and saw a family with three children sitting near me. They had two boys who looked like they might have been around twelve and fourteen, and a little girl who looked like she was about three. The little girl had Down Syndrome and, for some reason, was quite taken with me. We laughed and played together in whatever shade we could find until it was time for us to go through the gate. Her family seemed very pleased that their daughter had found a playmate to help with the boredom of waiting. I felt guilty leaving them behind but saw them later in the border terminal. I was so happy for them.

We sat in the crowded terminal, but at least we were out of the blazing sun. I talked to women who sat near me. They loved to practice their English with me as much as I appreciated their friendly faces in this place so far from home. We handed in our passports as soon as we entered the building, and had to wait to hear our names called to indicate that our passports had been processed, our visas were issued, and we could be on our way to Gaza!

This was the tricky part. There was no way of knowing how long our passports would be held but, honestly, we didn't care. Just making it this far, we knew that, no matter how long we sat there, we were going to end our day in Gaza. Sitting here was as good as making it across, almost. It was hard to understand what the agents were saying since they had such heavy Arabic accents so we listened very carefully every time a name was called out. Since we were a group of four, we had no idea whose name would be called first, so we all paid attention.

It felt like we were waiting for ages, but as soon as our names were called, the time seemed to be nothing at all as we happily jumped up to claim our passports and proceed on our way. We pushed our luggage down the last few metres, paid for our Palestinian visas and walked outside to catch the bus that would bring us over to the Palestinian border terminal. All four of us could hardly contain our excitement. We all knew that getting into Gaza was the closest thing to impossible that any of us had known, but here we were, in the final step of getting in. This trip had gone so much more smoothly than any of us had imagined. I was so grateful.

One ♥ Try

Hamoudi was waiting, and we were almost there.

Hamoudi had his cameraman, Khader, with him to record every bit of our reunion! When we walked out of the terminal, and Hamoudi and I finally were together again, we couldn't believe our eyes. The moment was as beautiful as it was surreal. We laughed and hugged and then stood back just to take each other in. It was so good to be back there finally and it was absolutely amazing to be with Hamoudi again. All of my efforts and agonies had been worth it. All of the pain of my last visit fell away into oblivion. I didn't even remember it anymore. It was as if none of those terrible times ever happened.

Hamoudi arranged a taxi for our three friends and he and I took a car by ourselves that Khader drove. We talked excitedly all the way from Rafah back to Gaza City. He had already set up a flat for us to stay in and arranged for our friends to stay in a flat in the same building we were in. We had planned for me to stay for about six months, or until Hamoudi had been granted his resident visa to come to Canada. We were finally together after being married for just over a year, and being apart for all but three weeks of that time.

As we entered our home, I was overwhelmed at the realization that we were finally together. The road had been very rocky, frustrating and painful, but God had continued to open doors and windows to keep me moving forward to this moment.
I settled in to life in Gaza fairly well. My children and I chatted online every day that we could. It meant that I would wake up any time between four and six a.m. to accommodate their evening schedule, but I didn't mind at all. I just needed to see them.

It was summer in Gaza, so it was very hot; much hotter than I was used to with summers in western Canada. Fortunately, I had brought light clothing with me but I was still hot and sweaty every day.

Hamoudi was still working as a TV reporter with Xinhua, a Chinese news agency that had an office in Gaza. He insisted that I stay home and let him work and support us. That sounded like a good idea except that his days were often long and I needed to interact with the people of Gaza while I was there. I needed to get to know people in order to reach out to them and share my love with them. God had brought me a long way, through a lot of trouble and I couldn't see that I had come all this way to spend all of my days closed in our flat.

I had led a humanitarian delegation to work with children and youth – and that's what I needed to do.

I talked to Hamoudi to find out where I could work and he made a few suggestions; mostly aid organizations and a school. I emailed all of them and heard back from only one; The American International School. This school was right down the street from us, which made it the most convenient place for me to get to.

The thought of being able to give back to a group of students, teachers and administrators that had suffered so much with having their previous school building bombed flat was overwhelming for me. God had brought me to this place with a heart full to give where I could in whatever way was needed. As I reflected on my first visit to the American International School in June 2009, I was excited to think that perhaps I could share in the lives of the people for whom I had already come to care so much for. I would have been happy to hear from anyone that I had contacted regarding working in Gaza, but secretly, I hoped, most of all, to hear from this school that had already impacted me so much.

I went to the school to introduce myself and to meet the administrators, Mr. Ribhi Salem and Dr. Mohammed Owdaa. As I sat in the office, I met Lucy, the secretary, and her sister, Nancy. They were sisters and they were Christians. I was so excited! I told them that I wanted to reach Gaza's Christians and was so happy to meet them so soon after arriving.

My conversation with Mr. Ribhi and Dr. Owdaa was better than I could have expected. Both men were happy to have me there and recognized what value I had to give to their students. I was hired by that school to work with the students on their English fluency and they gave me the opportunity to work with children from grades kindergarten to grade twelve. I was with children every day and I was allowed to talk about anything I wanted in the classroom, as long as it was in English. I missed my own children terribly, but being around these kids all the time helped ease the ache in my heart. I soon grew to love my students deeply as I opened up to them and dove into my work there.

I wanted to know more about their lives and their feelings about living in Gaza. I had grown accustomed to hearing the sounds of Israeli fighter jets and bombing but it was mostly in the distance. Until the night that Hamoudi and I were sitting together, watching TV. Suddenly there was a loud BOOM and a flash lit up the building across the street from us. I jumped, threw my arms around Hamoudi and shouted. Then I began to cry. That was too loud and too close for me to just let it pass as part of the normal background sounds of Gaza.

Hamoudi held me until I calmed down and started laughing. He teased me for getting to upset over just one bomb dropping. He, of course, had lived through so much worse than a single bomb dropping. We learned later that a Hamas security facility that was about three or four blocks away had been hit. It is not uncommon for buildings that are in the middle of residential areas to be bombed by Israel F-16's flying overhead. This one event was scary enough for me.

Working with the kids at school helped me gain a better perspective of life there. I learned from them how to not let any of the peripheral noises get me down. I learned how to just live normally, laugh and play. I learned that even with bombs dropping regularly, I could still care about the everyday stuff of life like, what we would eat for dinner, when we could go shopping, where I could buy notebooks and paper for school.

These kids live under unspeakable pressure, but they still behave like regular kids. I found myself loving them even more.

With my high school students, I had them write essays and give speeches. I encouraged them to say whatever was on their minds and to use their imaginations. I learned that use of the imagination was a challenge in Gaza.

I remember the day I asked one of my classes to write a page on what they would do if they had a day free to go wherever they wanted and to do whatever they wanted for that day. One of my girls put up her hand and said, "My mom doesn't let me out to do whatever I want." I smiled and said again, "Imagine, sweetheart. Pretend how it would be IF you could go and do anything." It took a minute for my suggestion to sink in and take hold, and finally I could see the light go on in her eyes. She could finally imagine that kind of freedom.

I was advised by the kindergarten teacher that just reading stories to the little ones was enough. They just needed to hear a foreign language and learn that it could be friendly. The foreign language most of them were used to hearing was Hebrew, and their experience wasn't a good one. They needed to know that some foreigners were good and meant them no harm.

I read stories to children up to grade three but with the older of those grades, I would ask questions after I finished reading to make sure they understood what I had said.

One day when I was in the grade three class, a group of F-16's buzzed overhead. I stopped reading and looked at all the little faces in front of me. Every child was frozen with their eyes to the sky, waiting, as I was, to see if those planes were going to drop anything on us. I quickly did a mental review of all the emergency preparations I had learned, and soon realized that I had only learned what to do in case of an earthquake. I had no idea what to do in case of a bombing. I kept thinking, "Get the kids under their desks and stand in the doorway. Stay away from the windows". Then I would remind myself again, "No, no! That won't help if they bomb us!"

I realized that the best I could give these little children was to help them not be afraid. I was terrified so I prayed quickly and asked God for strength and wisdom to get through this moment.

God provided. I took a deep breath, smiled at the class and said, "Wow! What a big noise! Let's get back to our story" and I continued reading "Cloudy With a Chance of Meatballs", making funny voices for all the characters. As I read, I had a part of my mind on the sky, and part of my mind praying that there was no reason to keep my mind on the sky. I felt most proud of myself a few days later when we were buzzed by F-16's again. This time I wasn't with the grade three class, they were with their regular teacher. I spoke to her later that day and she told me that her students spoke of nothing else for the rest of the day. I thought back to the day that I was with them, and how quickly we were able to forget about the planes. I realized that I had been able to give the children peace of mind that day, in the middle of a very frightening day. This is why I came to Gaza. I wanted to somehow bring comfort to the kids there. On that day, I had done just that.

I came home and had dinner ready for Hamoudi everyday when he got home from work. The food in Gaza is limited, so we ended up eating pasta and meat sauce almost every day, but Hamoudi loved it. This was the first time I had cooked for him, so he enjoyed every bite. Our life was as "normal" as it would be anywhere. We both worked and came home at the end of the day and got up the next morning to do it all again. I loved it when he came home. Every time he walked through that door it was like a special treat not to be taken for granted. We had waited so long for this.

I arrived in Gaza on August tenth, and started working at the school at the beginning of September. I have never worked in the classroom full time before, so it took some effort for me to get used to it. Coming home every night to Hamoudi made everything easier to handle. I attended Gaza Baptist Church where one of the ESL teachers also attended. I felt at home. I felt like this was my community. With Hamoudi's long hours, I made a point to learn where everything was in our neighbourhood; the pharmacy, the grocery store, the pizza shop, and the hair dresser. It didn't take long before I could get anywhere I needed to fairly quickly and easily.

September rolled into October, and I was welcoming the cooler nights. Gaza is so hot that I was looking forward to being able to get through a day without sweating. I was getting more settled into our routine. Working with the school kids was amazing. It was even better than I had dreamed it would be. The feedback from the parents left me speechless. They told me that I had given their children something they hadn't been given before; a place to speak their minds and be free to express their feelings. I was overjoyed. I had come to this land to share God's love with the people here and I was touching families by opening my heart to these children in my care. I couldn't ask for more than this.

Near the end of October, I had to ask Hamoudi to call in sick for me. I couldn't get out of bed, not even to make the necessary call. I was sure that by spending that day in bed, I would be fine to go to work the next day. Neither Hamoudi nor I would have ever imagined what was to happen next.

For the **Love** of Hamoudi

Chapter Ten

Honey, There's a Fly in My Couscous

The next day dawned worse than the day before. I still thought I had the flu but it was getting a stronger hold of me. I still felt weak and I was also getting a headache. I stayed in bed, and Hamoudi stayed home to watch me. He could tell I wasn't doing very well, so he stayed with me. He didn't leave me to go to work the next day. From that moment forward, he spent every minute taking care of me.

My headache quickly became unbearable and my fever spiked to forty degrees Celsius. No matter what he tried, Hamoudi was unable to get my fever down. He called for two different doctors to come to our home. They both gave him medications to help get my fever down. Neither worked. Hamoudi took me to a clinic to see a doctor in Gaza. We lived on the third floor of our building so I had to walk down all the stairs to the ground floor, and back up again when we got home. In my memory, I see endless stairs, but it was only three floors. As I look back, I can't believe I was able to get up and down those stairs. I was so sick and weak.

At home, I was running to the bathroom to vomit, and I'd try to get back to bed so I could lie down. I would no sooner get into bed when I'd have to run to the bathroom again. It was exhausting. One of the times that I was staggering back to bed, I mumbled to Hamoudi, "I don't know how much more of this I can take."

I didn't know what was wrong with me, but the symptoms were quickly wearing me out. My head felt like it was going to split open and my stomach refused to calm down. The only thing I could get down was cold water, but even that would immediately come up again. No matter what medication we tried, my fever was raging. Hamoudi made sure there was always ice in the freezer so he could cool me with the coldest cloths possible. He would put cloths on my head, torso and legs. By the time he got my legs covered, the cloth on my head would be hot; not warm, but hot. He would start again. He kept covering me in ice cold cloths but still, my fever would not let go. We didn't know what we were dealing with, but Hamoudi would not give up.

I remember telling him, after he took my temperature again and, again, it remained at forty degrees, "My brain is cooking, you know". Even as I said the words, they terrified me. I knew that I was losing this fight, but I didn't want to say it like that. Hamoudi was trying as hard as he could, but we could not break this fever. As I lay there, I thought of my five children in Canada. They didn't know anything about my illness yet at this point. In fact, I didn't even know much about my illness. Hamoudi and I were still in reaction mode, trying to cope with the symptoms without being able to get any clear diagnosis yet.

Hamoudi finally made the decision to move me to his father's home. He was getting exhausted with providing round the clock nursing care. His step mom was a nurse so he felt it would be better if I was in her care instead. Hamoudi called another doctor to come and look at me while I was at his dad's home, and that doctor advised that I be immediately transferred to the hospital. He called the ambulance and when they arrived, the attendants loaded me onto a chair and carried me down four flights of stairs, down to the street. I don't remember this very clearly at all. The only thing I remember is being terrified with every step they took because I thought I was going to fall. Hamoudi held my hand all the way. He was heartbroken to see so much fear in my eyes. When we got to the hospital, I was moved into a bed in the Emergency Department. There, the doctor wanted to get a blood sample to test to try to figure out what they were dealing with. They tried my right arm and couldn't find a vein. They tried my left arm, which usually has a nice big vein, but couldn't find anything they could use on that arm either. Their only possible point to get a blood sample was to go into my femoral artery. When the doctor told me this, it made me realize just how serious my condition was. I was told that putting a needle into me in my upper thigh would be very painful, so I should brace myself. I thought that if I was far enough gone that they needed to use my femoral artery, I need to just toughen up and put up with whatever pain might go with this procedure. My life depended on it, of that I was sure. Again, I lay and thought about my children and Hamoudi. I knew I was slipping away, and I couldn't stop it. I love them all so much, and here I was, leaving them and I didn't even know why. It was shortly after this point that I lost consciousness. I only know what happened because Hamoudi told me later. He had to leave with the blood samples that had finally been taken from me and rush them to a local lab for testing. When he returned to the hospital to be back at my side, he was pushed out of the room as soon as he tried to enter.

He only had a split second to see that I was on the floor and the doctors were frantically doing CPR on me. His step mom, Hanan, was crying uncontrollably as I lay on the floor, unresponsive, my face blue and my mouth foaming. Hamoudi's dad pushed him out of the room and told him that there was nothing he could do at that moment.

After this, Hamoudi contacted the Red Cross and the Canadian Embassy. I have no memory of anything that happened during this time but I know that whatever he did worked and I woke up, many days later, in a hospital in Tel Aviv, Israel.

I later learned that a doctor in Gaza had taken Hamoudi aside and given him the "we did all we could do" speech. He didn't have any expectation that I would survive, and he wanted Hamoudi to learn to come to terms with the fact. Once in Tel Aviv, when the doctor checked my temperature and saw that it was still forty degrees, he told Hamoudi that my brain was cooking. Immediately, Hamoudi remembered me saying the same thing several days earlier, and shuddered. The doctors in Tel Aviv didn't expect me to recover either.

I later learned that I had developed something called occipital lesions, which are lesions on the occipital lobe of my brain and can create some wild hallucinations. I remember some things from that time. I knew I was in a hospital, but I thought I was in Vancouver. I could hear Hamoudi's voice telling me that we're in Tel Aviv and I would laugh inside thinking, "Oh my goodness! He thinks we're in Tel Aviv! There's no way we're in Tel Aviv; he's going to freak out if I tell him we're actually in Vancouver." Of course, there was no way I could have told Hamoudi that we were in Vancouver since I had not yet regained consciousness.

I remember seeing out the door of my room into the hallway. I kept seeing a young Arab male nurse walking back and forth. He would barely look at me but would wave and smile a little. Behind him, I saw a lottery booth just like the ones that are all over the place at home. This is the reason I thought I was in Vancouver. I also "saw" a sign on the wall that I thought was a kind of word puzzle. Where there should be letters, there were only sticks, I thought. It looked like the kind of game that you would have to shake and try to get the sticks to make letters. Since I was in bed and obviously couldn't get up to shake the picture frame, I thought I could shake my head and solve the puzzle. I couldn't move any part of me but thought I was squeezing my eyes shut and shaking my head. Every time I would do this, I would "see" that the puzzle would be solved, in a different way each time. Although the words would always be different, it was always an encouraging phrase, such as "You can get through this", "keep fighting, you can make it", and many similar messages. I learned much later that these signs were actually reminders for the hospital staff to wash their hands! The signs were all written in Hebrew, which looks very much like sticks intersecting at crazy angles.

I had many strange thoughts while I was unconscious, including the thought that I was on a yacht or a mansion or something like that. I never saw the people who owned the place; I only ever heard their voices. My surroundings were luxurious, which is the reason I thought I was on a yacht or in a mansion. I never saw any people, but heard many voices discussing investing and all the voices had a Filipino accent, which I found very comforting. I relaxed in the knowledge that I was in good hands. I was unable to move anything from my head to my toes and I was not able to utter any sounds, but I was aware of the fact that I was aware of myself, so I knew I was alive.

I was comforted by this understanding. I knew that as long as my brain was alive, the rest of me had a chance to recover. I was briefly upset when I realized that I had no ability to speak. For me to lose that was an enormous loss, and yet, I experienced only a minor disturbance over this. As long as I could think, Hamoudi could be my voice if I needed him to be. Thinking was the most important thing, and I was able to do that. Everything else would be alright.

God gave me incredible calm during what could have been a very frightening time. I knew that He had given me life, and whatever else came with it would be an extra blessing.

When I finally woke up in the ICU of the hospital in Tel Aviv, all of the doctors and nursing staff came to my bed to congratulate me and tell me that they were happy to see me. They also told me that they never expected me to wake up, and were surprised when I did.

I couldn't reply to them, and when I tried, I would always start coughing unless I just mouthed the words without even a whisper. Hamoudi would lean close to me and put his ear close enough to my mouth so he could hear what I was saying and tell the person I was trying to talk to. Everyone else would just say they didn't know why I couldn't talk. Hamoudi was my voice during that time.

I learned later that I had been intubated for several days and that had damaged my vocal chords. I learned that my throat would eventually recover, but it would be a while before my voice would return to normal. I still have a scar on my lip and beside my mouth from having the tubing in place for so long. I had no idea why I couldn't speak or how long I would be like this. At first, I thought that my voice was just gone. When I started being able to make some sounds, my voice was very raspy and quiet. I tried singing and no sound would come out at all. I was a little sad for that. It's not like I'm a good singer or anything, but I always loved singing to my kids, and that was no longer possible. My voice has since fully recovered, and I speak normally except for some of the other effects of this illness.

It turned out that I had encephalitis, which is a fever of the brain. For people who get as sick as I did, full recovery is very rare. It is absolutely miraculous that God returned me to health and abilities almost the same as before I got sick.

Honey, There's a Fly in **My** Couscous

When I first woke up and tried to talk, I couldn't remember anything that I wanted to say. I'd say a couple of words and forget what I wanted to say next. Another after-effect that I notice is that sometimes my words don't come out clearly. I have been told I have a slight slur sometimes. I am not afraid to speak, but am a bit self conscious when I notice that my words start sticking together a bit. My eye sight suddenly got worse, which I also read is an expected effect of this illness.

When I was learning to walk again, I first had to use a walker. I would force my legs to cooperate as I made my way up and down the halls of the hospital. It was pretty scary at first because I felt like I was going to fall down. My physiotherapist told me, at that point, if I did fall down, it would set me back to the beginning of my recovery. My infection was gone, but the road to my physical recovery is long and, at times, very difficult.

Because encephalitis leaves you with an acquired brain injury, there are some effects that don't seem to make sense but that I have to deal with anyways. A brain injury affects me emotionally. I cry more easily, get angry more easily, and sometimes over react to things that go on around me. This frustrates me and I find myself asking God why He ever let me get sick in the first place but I have found, as when I have gone through difficulties in the past, that the experience has taught me to be more compassionate and understanding of others.

I believe that I am always in His hands, and even when I was at my lowest point and not expected to recover, His hands were under me, sustaining me, keeping me and ready to lift me up again.

God gave us more miracles besides restoring my life and health. Because of the seriousness of my condition, Hamoudi was allowed out of Gaza and into Israel. As a Palestinian man who is under thirty-five years old, this is impossible. And yet, he was granted permission. Hamoudi stayed by my side while I was recovering in Tel Aviv. The hospital food was almost unbearable so he kept running to bring me food. Without eating, I could not regain my strength, but with the food they served, I could not eat. Hamoudi helped me get stronger.

One day, my meal tray was delivered, as usual, to my bedside. As I pulled it closer, trying to figure out what I had been given, I noticed that a small fly was firmly stuck in my couscous. Try as he might, he could not get his feet free. I was horrified. I waved my hand as fast as I could over the fly, hoping to scare him away, but no matter how vigorously I swatted at him, the fly couldn't go anywhere. Hamoudi noticed my flapping and came over to ask me what was wrong.

"Honey, there's a fly in my couscous!" Even as the words left my mouth, I realized how funny that sounded and Hamoudi and I laughed and laughed. Of course, no matter how funny it was, there was no way at all that I was going to be eating that meal! Hamoudi quickly removed my tray, complete with the poor captive fly, and ran to get me something else to eat. Of course, part of life in the hospital is being able to shower when necessary. Because my movement was severely restricted, I needed help with everything at first. A tall Russian nurse took me down the hall in my wheel chair for my first shower since waking up. I was looking forward to feeling fresh again.

She backed me up into the shower stall and got ready. Suddenly, she started hosing me down to get me wet. She sprayed me right in the face; I couldn't breathe. I was not able to raise my arms to my shoulders, and certainly not any higher, so I was completely helpless to cover my face as she continued to spray me. I struggled for breath and tried to turn my head but I could not escape. She just looked at me with a smug, stern look and kept spraying.

I felt like I was some kind of farm animal being washed off with a hose. It was a humiliating procedure.

After she was finally finished, I was determined never to let her help me again. The next time I needed a shower, I was still unable to raise my arms, so I asked another nurse if should would please help me. She was a kind and gentle Arabic nurse and, although we didn't speak each others' languages fluently, she sensed my fear and desperation and agreed to help me for my next shower.

I felt human again, a very helpless human, but at least I was treated with dignity this time.

After that, I decided that by the time I was to shower again, I would do it myself. As I lay in my bed, I worked with my arms, forcing them higher and higher until I could finally reach my ears. In order to wash my hair, I would need to reach the top of my head but I noticed that if I leaned my head right over on each shoulder, I could almost reach the top of my head. That was close enough for me!

On my next shower day I pulled my walker over to the side of my bed and pulled myself up. Then I slowly and carefully walked down the hall of my hospital ward until I made it to the shower room. By this time I was exhausted and I had only begun my mission!

The shower I took that day was possibly the longest I've ever taken and it was, for sure, the most work. When I was all finished, I proudly made my way back to my room and laid down for a nap. I was so tired, but happy that I had accomplished this important task all of my own. Recovery was very difficult, but I was determined not to have to rely on others for my personal care.

As I was recovering, I started noticing that my right arm had an itchy rash all over it and I was also itchy all over my legs and torso. The doctors attending to me were puzzled, so they started giving me an antihistamine to get rid of the rash. Finally, I figured out what was causing this problem. I am allergic to latex, and all of the hospital staff wore latex gloves. I was also told that all of the IV tubes were made of latex, and my right arm was mostly used for my IV's. I told one of the doctors about my allergy and asked her to please tell the staff since they don't all speak English and I don't speak Russian or Hebrew, the languages that most of the staff spoke.

In spite of my efforts to alert the staff to my allergy, no one stopped wearing latex gloves around me, and my rash became worse. Finally, I begged the doctor to order latex-free gloves to be worn around me. She called the hospital pharmacy and found that they didn't even carry latex-free gloves. Instead, we were advised to go to the retail pharmacy across the street from the hospital to buy our own latex-free gloves. Hamoudi went to buy them but even that pharmacy didn't carry them. We were exasperated because my itchy rash just kept getting worse because of my continued exposure to latex. Finally, Hamoudi went to the local McDonald's and asked for some of the plastic gloves they use for food preparation. When he explained why he needed them, the girl gave him a whole box of them for me! I put them on my bedside table and asked the doctor to tell all the staff that I now had latex-free gloves, and I needed everyone to use them. No one did. Instead, they increased my antihistamines to try to deal with my worsening rash.

Honey, There's a Fly in **My** Couscous

Hamoudi was beside me when I had to take my first increased dose of antihistamines. As it happened, the medication was too strong for my stomach, and I started throwing up. I was terrified. It was like the beginning of my illness all over again. I looked at the nurses and asked, desperately, "Why am I throwing up?" They just shrugged their shoulders. I couldn't help but think that I was too weak to survive another bout of encephalitis. I wouldn't make it this time. I sat on my bed as my body kept heaving, crying and begging for help.

Hamoudi stepped in close to me and said, "It's your medication, baby. It's too strong for you. Don't worry, you'll be ok. It's just your medication."

His words made perfect sense to me and soothed me immediately. In my worst moments of fear, he was always there, holding my hand, smoothing my hair, making me believe I'd be alright.

When the nurse came later to give me my increased dose of antihistamines and handed me the pills with her latex gloved hand, I refused the medication. I told her that her glove was the reason I had to take medication, and that it was making me sick. It was time for me to go home.

I had been making good progress with my recovery, but had been going backwards over the last few days. I had been eating fairly well, but had all but stopped eating again. I had begun to walk, but was now hardly even getting out of bed. As I looked over these facts, I began to get scared, wondering if perhaps I had not beaten this illness, after all.

After much analysis, I figured out that I was getting depressed; I needed to be home and have my kids around me. I begged Hamoudi to try to get me released. The Canadian embassy had given Hamoudi permission to come home with me because I was too weak to travel alone, and Israel had given him permission to leave the country through the Ben Gurion airport, something that Palestinians were generally not allowed to do. My parents had made all the arrangements with Air Canada to book us a flight home, and now all we needed was for the hospital to release me; but since my condition had begun to deteriorate again, they were reluctant to issue my release.

Hamoudi went to the nurses' station to discuss our departure with them, and while he was there, I lay in bed, worrying about what was taking him so long. I pulled myself out of bed and carefully made my way down the hall to where he was standing. I leaned against the countertop and begged the nurse to arrange for my release. Much to my surprise, I broke down crying, telling them how much I needed to be with my kids again.

Hamoudi turned and gently told me that everything was ok. He urged me to go back to my bed and relax. He would take care of everything. I went back to bed and laid down, being exhausted from my short trip. He came back to my room and told me we'd be leaving the next day. Again, he had been my rescuer and my support. God blessed me over and over again through Hamoudi.

We spent one night at a beautiful hotel outside the hospital. Early the next morning, we were picked up by two security officers from the Canadian embassy. It was an interesting experience for us. They were armed but very friendly. They drove us to the airport and stayed with us until we passed through security to wait for our flight home.

It was not the trip I had expected. I thought I would stay with Hamoudi and live in Gaza working with the children there for several months. Instead, I only worked with the kids for two months, got sick, and had to leave without being able to tell anyone. Without being able to go back to Gaza to say any Good Bye's, I now had to board a plane and leave it all behind. Hamoudi and I got on our plane and flew to Canada. When we arrived in Toronto, and rushed through the airport to catch our connecting flight to Vancouver, I became aware of the Christmas music being played over the sound system, and of the Christmas decorations hanging around the airport.

"I made it home for Christmas!" suddenly flooded my mind! In my time in the hospital, I had lost all track of time, and dates, and everything. I had no idea that it was almost Christmas time. I would be with my kids for Christmas, after all. Tears filled my eyes as my heart was filled with gratitude that God had delivered me, alive and home for Christmas.
Hamoudi and I still have the challenge of his immigration to deal with. After all we've been through, we are not afraid of the next steps that lie ahead of us. God has shown His love and mercy to us in a very big way.

I have no idea what He has for me to do next except to recover and rest. My kids are thrilled to have me home, and to see that I'm getting better.

I'm now spending my days making sure I get a nap if I want to do something exciting, which is a rhythm that takes some getting used to. I am waiting on God to open the next door – and I know He has one.

For the **Love** of Hamoudi

Chapter Eleven

For the Love of Hamoudi

It was for the love of Hamoudi that God introduced me to a whole new world and taught me how to truly be a good neighbour.

I am moved to tears by Stephen Sizer's telling of the Parable of the Good Samaritan. He points out that Jesus explained that the wounded man was "naked and half dead". As Stephen points out, this means that no one could determine the man's racial or ethnic identity by his clothing or by his accent. He was naked and unconscious. No one knew if he was "one of us or one of them". The man in the road was a human first. Jesus was talking about treating people as humans – period. He was the front runner of respecting human rights. I had been given an opportunity to be a neighbour to people who are often seen as "them". Loving your neighbour works better when you actually get to know them.

It was for the love of Hamoudi that God showed me what I was capable of when I gave it all to Him. I would have never thought that I would lead a humanitarian delegation and fall in love with many of Gaza's children and youth and have the wonderful opportunity of giving them my heart and loving them with the love of God that flows through me.

It was for the love of Hamoudi that God taught me to love a nation of people. God has equipped and enabled me to be a voice for peace and justice where such a voice is desperately needed.

For the **Love** of Hamoudi

It was for the love of Hamoudi that God allowed me to create a bridge with my Palestinian brothers and sisters in Christ. Again, it's so much easier to really love people when you take the time and make the effort to get to know them.

If I've learned anything, it's that anything truly is possible, even the impossible becomes possible when you throw it all into God's hands and trust Him for the outcome. If I had believed that the outcome was up to me, I would still be struggling. By releasing my dreams, my vision and my hopes into His capable hands, it was all returned to me together with everything necessary for it to all happen.

My journey of faith into the Gaza Strip became so much more than I dared to expect. My life is changed, my joy has been increased to a remarkable measure and my heart has been broken in ways that will keep me hungry and moving forward, pressing for more love for a people who are so unloved by so many in my part of the world.

I could have spent my whole life staying at home and minding my own business. I could have just focused on my life and no one would have criticized me for that. I am so grateful that God had a different plan for me!

I would encourage anyone to dare to care about people that we are not expected to care about. Dare to care enough to be moved out of our comfort zones and step into the real world.

I learned that it's only when I let go and open my hands to God's blessings that He has room to do amazing things in my life. I had always felt inadequate, unequipped, and of course, I was as long as I struggled to work everything out on my own. By leaning on God and giving Him my life and my future, He led in ways I never could have. He led me to places I never could have gone and he equipped me in ways that were more exciting than I ever could have dreamed of! What I have is more than adequate to meet the challenges that God brings in front of me because He has filled me with strength and the faith I need to always move forward.

There are times when it feels like I'm sitting still, especially during my recovery period, but even as I feel that I'm not "doing" anything, I am constantly being encouraged by the progress as I regain my physical abilities.

I can now speak clearly, shower normally, and walk normally, just not always as far as I'd like to. I still cannot run or jump, but I probably wasn't too good at that anyways!

For the love of Hamoudi, my life has been changed. I have met some wonderful people and accomplished things that are much too big for someone "like me". I have learned, much to my joy, that God specializes in using ordinary people to achieve extraordinary things in life!

I am ordinary. And yet, I have an extraordinary story.

For the **Love** of Hamoudi

LANGLEY SECONDARY SCHOOL

École Secondaire Langley

21405 - 56th Avenue
Langley, British Columbia V2Y 2N1
e-mail: lssinfo@sd35.bc.ca
Telephone: 604-534-4171
Fax: 604-534-9518

"Nothing Without Effort"

To Whom It May Concern:

It comes with great pleasure that I have the opportunity to write this letter of appreciation to Linda Gharib for her willingness to educate others and spread her passion for social change through individual action.

For two consecutive years, Linda has provided time in her life to come and speak about her worthy cause in my Social Justice class at Langley Secondary School. Her discussion involves the education about a world crisis and having the students create an individualistic view while keeping the principles of social justice as the backdrop. The students are always engaged by her passion and her adventures and experiences. She truly is dedicated to her cause.

Every semester I teach social justice 12, which includes a learning outcome of social action. I desire to have Linda speak as a Canadian citizen who not only has taken a keen interest into international human rights violations, but has also found a way to participate in social change. Linda has come to speak to my class three times over the past two years and I hope to see her again in the upcoming years. Her story is truly an inspiration to us all to have fidelity to a cause we believe in, no matter the risks and the difficulty.

Respectfully,

Michael Carlyle

M.Ed B.Sc

Langley Secondary School Educator

Langley Secondary School is dedicated to providing a learning environment of cooperation and respect in which students prepare to meet the intellectual, career and social challenges of the future.

For the **Love** of Hamoudi

unrwa
الأونروا

60

united nations relief and
works agency for palestine
refugees in the near east

tatram gaza field office
jamal abad el naser street
p.o. box 61
gaza
or
p.o. box 731
ashqelon
israel
+972 8 2887333

+972 8 2887444
+972 8 2887445

www.unrwa.org

27 June 2010

UR 10-526

To Whom It May Concern,

UNRWA is pleased to invite Ms Linda Todd and her delegation to visit Gaza.

Ms. Todd and her delegation plan to enter Gaza in order to undertake work on the theme "Right to Read". The main purpose of their visit will be to support education in Gaza, including for children studying in UNRWA schools. They will volunteer at non-governmental organizations focused on children and literacy and record children's stories for publication and dissemination in their home countries of Canada, the United Kingdom and the USA.

All of the members of the delegation have experience working with children and youth of various ages.

We appreciate your efforts to facilitate their entry into Gaza.

Yours sincerely,

John Ging
Director of UNRWA Operations/Gaza

وكالة الأمم المتحدة
لإغاثة وتشغيل اللاجئين
الفلسطينيين في الشرق الأدنى
عزة
VAI
المصخل
اشدونل

+٩٧٢ ٨ ٢٨٨٧٣٣٣
+٩٧٢ ٨ ٢٨٨٧٤٤٤
+٩٧٢ ٨ ٢٨٨٧٤٤٥

167

For the **Love** of Hamoudi

Chapter Twelve

Articles, Resources & Reading

Some of my thoughts while I was in Gaza

Today one of my classes started making some artwork that will be displayed over here in North America.

I told them to draw how they feel about living in Gaza. What do they see? What is a memory that keeps coming to mind?

As they drew, they started talking . . .

One very sweet, bright boy told me the story of one of his friends. The boy's father was arrested by the Israelis for something and he was killed. The father of his sister's friend was also arrested by the Israelis, this time for burning an Israeli flag at the end of the war. He was taken, murdered, and then his body was wrapped in a blanket and delivered to the doorstep of his home. The ones who delivered the body knocked and walked away.

The wife and daughter of the deceased man came to the door and found something wrapped in a blanket. They pulled the blanket back to find it was the father of this family. I could hardly breathe, imagining such a horror.

Another boy told me that in the first day of the war, Israeli soldiers entered his home and broke everything. "Why did they break it?", he asked. Of course, I had no answer. He went on to tell me that there were people being killed all around where he lived, including women and children, and that when the ambulances came, the soldiers would let them take out the dead bodies but not allow them to rescue the injured.

I wanted to cry.

We just can't imagine what these children have witnessed. These kids are in grade six now, so they were in grade four when all of that happened. Some of the kids weren't finished yet, so I told them they could finish next Sunday. One of my students asked if she could also write something for me to publish so I told her she could.

One of my girls called me over to her and told me quietly that the Israelis are planning to attack again but no one knows when. I told her I had heard that too. She said softly, "It makes me afraid".

PLEASE impress upon people what these children have suffered and the ongoing psychological terrorism that continues. A few days ago, Israel held "mock airstrikes" during our first period.

Last night they bombed somewhere for real. They are always bombing and you can tell when they are close because many of the younger children show up to school the next day looking completely haggard and worn out. The dark circles around their eyes show their lack of sleep. It is barbaric for Israel to continue to terrorize these children.

I woke up at four this morning and didn't know why until I got to school today and learned about last night's bombing. It was at four am. I must have been sleeping deeply enough not to hear it but not so deeply that I was able to sleep through it.

The children are afraid because the images of the last war, of all the death and fear, are still so fresh in their minds.

Gaza's Precious Treasures

It's a new school year and Gaza has a new teacher —me. I have the awesome privilege of feeding young minds from kindergarten to grade twelve at the American International School in Gaza.

During my first class with the grade six students, I encouraged the children to introduce themselves to me. I wanted them to tell me a little about themselves. Child after child gave me their name and a few personal details as we all got to know each other a little better. Every child is beautiful, bright and angelic in their own way.

Finally, it was time for the girls to my left to introduce themselves to me. The first girl, with a thick blonde ponytail, bright hazel eyes and a gorgeous smile asked in her sweet voice, "Can I talk about the war?"

I was caught off guard, not expecting such words to come out of such an innocent face. I paused to catch my breath, not wanting these children to know that tears were almost filling my eyes.

I softly said, "Yes, if you want to."

For the **Love** of Hamoudi

She proceeded to tell me about the first day of bombing and how scary it was for her family to have bombs dropping all around her home. She told me, in vivid detail, where each member of her family was, how frantically her mother was trying to locate all of her children. She told me how terrified she was when her home was filled with smoke so no one could find each other, how they all called out for each other, hoping that everyone was alright.

I held my breath as I listened to her. This innocent child is the same age as my youngest son. As I heard her story, I thought of how I would feel if my own child was forced to live through such a nightmare. My mind was blank.

She continued her story for the next few minutes, taking me through every step of that first day, letting me relive it with her and suddenly she said, "And then it was over", and her story ended. I could breathe again. I was so grateful that this is now her version of the story. In spite of the detailed horror of that first day, the next thing that came to mind was "and then it was over".

I am truly and deeply blessed to share in the lives of some of Gaza's children. I hope I can give them something back to help them as they look forward in their young lives.

They are bright, intelligent and beautiful inside and out and I hope and pray that we can find the way to give them the very best.

It's the least we should do.

Resources & Reading

To learn more about the people and organizations I've talked about, you can find them here:

Linda's website - **www.lindatoddgharib.com**

Linda's Youtube channel - **www.youtube.com/user/canada2gaza**

Blog that contains many essays from Linda's students in Gaza and her thoughts - **lindatodd.wordpress.com**

Brother Andrew and **Al Janssen** – Light Force and God's Smuggler Open Doors International - **www.opendoors.org**

Rev. Alex Awad – Palestinian Memories
Dean of Students and full time instructor, Bethlehem Bible College, Bethlehem, Palestine and Pastor of East Jerusalem Baptist Church - **www.alexawad.org**

Dr. Hanna Massad – there are many articles to read to learn more about my dear brother Hanna. Here are two:

   www.christianitytoday.com/ct/2005/july/9.44.html
   www.comeandsee.com/modules.php?name=News&file =article&sid=981

The Shepherd Society – Bethlehem, Palestine; ministering to the needs of Palestinians - **www.shepherd-society.org**

For donations from Canada, send them through
www.hopeoutreach.ca/index2.html

For the **Love** of Hamoudi

from the USA

Bethlehem Bible College (include for Shepherd Society in check memo). Send to: **Bethlehem Bible Co; 614-C South IH Bus. 35; New Braunfels, TX 78130**

Sami Awad – Executive Director of The Holy Land Trust

> **samiawad.wordpress.com**
> **www.holylandtrust.org**

You can find **Hamoudi** on Facebook!

www.facebook.com/people/Hamoudi-Ghareeb/772974537

For the **Love** of Hamoudi

ti

CPSIA information can be obtained at www.ICGtesting.com
Printed in the USA
BVOW071410191011

274049BV00001B/10/P